AMAZON TOP 50 BEST SELLING AUTHOR

DEAR VERONICA

April Crawford

Letters to and from a Spirit Guide

"Love is an expression of connection without any conditions."

Title: *"Dear VERONICA"*: Letters To And From A Spirit Guide

Author: April Crawford

Publisher: Connecting Wave
2629 Foothill Blvd.
Unit # 353
La Crescenta, CA 91214
www.ConnectingWave.com

ISBN: 978-0982326961

For Author Information: www.AprilCrawford.com

Other books via April Crawford: www.AprilCrawfordBooks.com

Book Design: Allen Crawford

For Permissions: Publisher@ConnectingWave.com

"Dear VERONICA" and "Inner Whispers" are trademarks.

Introduction

VERONICA is a highly evolved nonphysical entity and spirit guide that speaks, writes, consults, and physically visits with full body language via an Open Deep Trance Channel named April Crawford.

In addition to being a best selling author, April Crawford is one of the most gifted Open Deep Trance Channels and Spiritual Mediums in the world today, offering fully interactive two-way conversations with the "other side", all with zero "coloring" or distortion. Such is the nature of true deep trance work in this area.

Most of the live conversations are with highly evolved nonphysical entities and guides. Others... as with those in-between physical lives... can, and often do, also come through. However, for this particular book, as the title implies, it is the entity VERONICA that responds to all of the letters, except for one letter that April responds to directly.

The letters to VERONICA in this book were written by people from all around world. In each case, VERONICA responds specifically to the person who wrote the letter. However, it was VERONICA's intent to respond in a way that you may also relate to. Perhaps some of these letters will provide inspiration or knowledge that you will find helpful in your own personal life (and afterlife) situations.

For more information, including videos of VERONICA speaking while April is in deep trance, try www.AprilCrawford.com.

1

Dear VERONICA,

My name is Brenda and I am married and have 2 children. My daughter is 14 and my son is 10.

Over the past 3 or 4 year I have not felt the connection that I should with my husband. I believe that he feels the same way but neither one of us are willing to deal with it.

My husband has always felt that if things do not work in the bedroom nothing else matters. I on the other hand feel that in order to have a successful marriage or relationship, everything must work.

Thank you, Brenda

Dear Brenda,

In every relationship there is an ebb and flow to the energy of the two involved. This energy is not necessarily defined by the two in the exact same way. Both of you came into the relationship with different viewpoints encompassing far more than you shared in your note.

Realize that though your perspectives are different, there is a probable moment that could reconcile the differences you feel on a physical level.

The only way to reach this moment is through complete truth. There is much fear attached to the truth but if embraced, it will lead both of you to a better relationship.

Your children will also evolve more clearly by the example of truth. Decide how brave you are.

Perhaps your husband would welcome a frank discussion of what's impeding a harmonious relationship. Be truthful with him along with the acceptance of his truth.

You may be pleasantly surprised.

--VERONICA

2

Dear VERONICA,

re: divorce/loss.....how can I deal with the Love for my husband when he has now found his soul mate?

I wanted what they seem to have....but I cannot go back, too much betrayal ...have been moving forward except for this binding love I have for him....and him for me, as friends on his part.... Been a year and I'm much stronger, yet he's still constantly on my mind.... Been working on letting go - most my life.... any input?

Grateful. Thanks, Janet

Dear Janet,

This man has participated with you in many scenarios... not always pleasant. You will encounter him again perhaps when he becomes more evolved.

Letting go of an eternal connection can feel very wrong. It is necessary now in your current linear.

There are more than one Soulmate. We suggest his perceptions on the subject are limited.

Open your consciousness to the probability of meeting another "soul mate". There are a few. Remember that your energy (that is the true you) vibrates energetically with other souls. Look forward and keep your eyes "open".

The probability is high for a new encounter.

--VERONICA

3

Dear VERONICA,

My son Ryan was killed in a motorcycle accident recently.

He was only 22. My life has certainly changed since that day, and I am looking for positive meanings for all of this. It has been very difficult as a mother to lose a child. However, it has brought me to a much deeper understanding of the spirit world.

Ryan has spoken to me in dreams and shortly after his death he told me 'mom, in the end it will be all about love, love will be the most important thing you can do now. I have been doing a lot of reading on the subject of the spiritual world and I have noticed that quite a few spirits have told their loved ones the same thing.

Have you heard of this also? I am so fascinated by everything I am learning. I am no longer afraid to die and while I am here I want to be a much more loving and compassionate person.

Thanks for your time, Lisa

Dear Lisa,

Death is often a fearful subject. In this instance the death of a child poses a question to the parents supposedly left behind.

"Can I continue without the physical presence of the energy I gave birth to?"

The answer is yes!

The fine line between physical and spiritual is often transcended between parent and child in the death transition process. Your child is offering a moment of evolution that you have embraced, but after today will feel completely aligned with.

Feel his presence at all times. Your Ryan hovers about you. He will be the first energy you feel upon your own transition.

He hovers because he feels your energy attached to his continuance...... so he continues in a fashion recognizable to you.

He leaves you tangible markers of his continuance. Look for them. You are not imagining anything. It is all tangible. He is good and getting better.... the messages will become clearer and undeniable.

The rest of this existence for you will be filled with signs of his love.

It's an opportunity for advancement for both of you.

--VERONICA

4

Dear VERONICA,

Hello my name is Denise and I live in PA. Were do I start?

When I was 13 my great-grandmother passed away and when my family got home I went to bed and my mom and dad told me that they heard me talking to someone. It was my great grand mom.

Well from that day I can see ghosts and I had a couple of times were I would see my dead family. Like a couple of years ago my grandma (dad's mom) passed away after she got to hold my oldest child. I took that very hard.

Then about 5-7 years later my grand pop (dad's dad) passed away but when he did that day I could smell my grandma's perfume and that night at 9:30 pm my grand pop past away, but when he did I felt like someone took my breath away and his hand was on my shoulder.

That Friday my dad came to me and was going to tell me but I already knew. My husband and I moved in a house that we are renting and one day I was cleaning and I saw this tall dark looking man standing on my steps and he was in a marine suit and he had glasses on and when I went to look again he was gone.

I had to call my aunt and tell her, told her what I saw and she told me that was my uncle David. He was killed in a car accident 30 some years ago.

I have many things happen to me, I can go on and on.

Thank you for taking your time for reading this.

Denise

Dear Denise,

We feel the great energy inside of you that needed to write these experiences down on paper. The exercise itself was healing for you. Your sight is true, you are not making it up.

There is opportunity for more experience if you decide to open
yourself for it.

--VERONICA

5

Dear Veronica:

I saw the video clips, you mention "linear" a lot, what exactly does that mean, "linear"?

Sorry if this is a stupid question, but I want to make sure I understand.

Thank You.

> *Vero*

Dear Vero,

Linear is the perception of an experience in the physical. Usually a "lifetime" defined by a time line.

--VERONICA

6

Dear VERONICA,

Can you tell me who you were in your last life on earth?

What country, what year, and what gender you were?

Can I ask you if you have had a life in INDIA?
Thanks,

Deepak

Dear Deepak,

    We have been many in the physical. Our favorite life was in Bristol - Male in gender. Yes we have lived in India, however we remember all of our lives and the experiences that shape our current perspective.

    --VERONICA

7

Dear VERONICA,

I would like to know how do i keep the man I love by my side? He's my best friend. I really do feel comfortable with this man but for some reason sometimes I feel he's a little distant with me. I would like to know if you see any future with him or does he have another person in life or in the future? His name is Richard and his birthday is 04/14/XX.

Thank You.

Snow

Dear Snow,

   Keeping a relationship involves a delicate balance of yourself as you relate to him.

He also feels the comfortable sensing that is a result of your dual energy blend. The distance you feel is his own un-comfortableness and inner disappointment of his own actions and non actions.

To attempt to define his every nuance will only make you desperate. Realize that your energy will only attract him if it is strong. Keep your focus. Be the person who balances his energy.

The energy kept balanced will keep him in your sphere of reality. It is up to you. Whether you realize it or not the power is in your grasp.

-VERONICA

8

Dear VERONICA,

I have always believed in life after death and I was never disturbed by paranormal activity. But this time is different. You see Veronica, my father died 3 years ago and I always felt he was with us even though he never did mischievous things.

Now my mother sold the apartment where we lived over 30 years and where my father died. The new owners complain that my father doesn't let them live there. He is constantly opening doors, knocking on closets, and they actually feel like he is sitting next to them watching.

What can we do to stop this from happening and help this family live in peace?. They can't sleep and they have three small toddlers. I feel very bad for them and for my father that is in some kind of distress. They live overseas (Venezuela). Can you give me some advice?

Thank you Veronica. Maria

Dear Maria,

First of all the energy described does not feel like your father. He is at peace with his current environment.

This feels like an energy attached to those who currently inhabit the dwelling.

It may give them a sense of security to place the identity on that of your father. The responsibility is not yours.

We realize it is a male energy but not your father.

Your father sends his love and regards. He is currently creating another life for himself. He is <u>not</u> distressed.

-VERONICA

9

To Everyone:

Victim-hood is the coward's way out of one's own creation..."

"You may not always like what we say. However, it will always provoke you... that is our intention.

-VERONICA

10

Dear VERONICA,

My mother died this time last year.

The past year we have moved some of her furniture into our home. I have a dog that is two years old that my mom bought me. He is a precious Shi-tzu. Here recently he makes a habit of sitting on the end of my bed looking at the dresser. He will growl at you if you try to move him.

Her desk and chair have also been moved into my house.

Two nights in a row my husband and I have gone to get my dog to go to bed and he is sitting beside the chair at the desk just looking at it.

He will growl at you if you go to pick him up. It is like he is seeing something that is beyond my sight. I know that

animals and children see things that we do not see. Is he
seeing mother?

Lisa

Dear Lisa,

    He is conversing with your mother. We suggest you honor
that. He will be finished when he is finished.

        -VERONICA

11

Dear Veronica,

I'm a digital artist with some exciting career moves on the immediate horizon.......however, it is my heart that is tormented.

For over 5 years I have been involved with a man named David, a spiritual man, yet a fearful man. Though he has lost much in his life there is so much to gain for he and I together.

I know this man loves me. When will he free himself enough to let this happen? And what can I do in the meantime?

Thank You

Brenda

Dear Brenda,

The choice to intertwine energy with another in the physical is often wrought with stops and starts. Energy you must remember can be volatile especially within the physical existence.

The love between you is true. His fear is one of losing himself within that mixture. There are also past experiences that contribute to his disconnect.

You may never experience his full commitment in the terms that you have predefined. It's not for lack of love, merely his own issues.

Your decision to stay with him is your own. There is much to be gleaned in partnership with him. Be patient and alter your experience to align with the truth of the situation.

-VERONICA

12

Dear VERONICA,

My husband passed away 3 years ago Oct 30. He was in a nursing home for 3 years due to a rare brain disease. After he was in the home I met, and had a relationship with, a man whose wife was also in a home and suffered from the same disease as my husband.

It was a natural coming together of two souls who had such common ground.

Our relationship lasted two years and ended rather badly when he became involved with another.

I have not seen or heard from him in 3 years. Out of the blue he phoned me and asked if I was seeing anyone, which I am not, and he asked me out to dinner. I accepted. Our meeting seemed easy and natural.

Since the years have passed I have forgiven him and recovered from a "broken heart". I seem to be grounded *now and would like to approach this new encounter on a friendship basis.*

Would I be wise to try this approach, or am I again looking at being hurt? His wife still is living- still in the nursing home after 6 years. She is now confined to a wheelchair and no longer knows him.

Thanks for your consideration of my situation.

Carol

Dear Carol,

You are "good friends" on an energy level with this man. Keep your perceptions of him honest in your mind.

He seeks comfort. Give it to him without losing yourself in the process. Understand that it is not a romance but an energy exchange.

-VERONICA

13

Dear VERONICA

My husband and I have had a rough couple months. We got pregnant during our recent honeymoon. Everything was going along fine; we were able to see the heartbeat at our doctor visits and everything. After two months.... we lost the baby. According to the doctor, things weren't lining up genetically and it was natures way of letting it go.

I'm not telling you for sympathy but to express my interest in knowing At What Point Do Souls Enter the Body?

I feel like there is an entity out there that is trying to 'become' our child. My husband is heart broken (as am I) but he feels we need to come up with 'new' names next time around because 'that' baby didn't survive.

I feel differently..... the entity is still out there (the same one) but he/she is just waiting for a 'perfect entrance'.

Anyhow, I'm getting kinda personal but I figured I'd throw it out there. Maybe VERONICA can address this subject. I'm sure plenty of women and couples go through it.

-Anonymous [name omitted by request]

Dear Anonymous,

You have not participated in a neglectful way. In other words it wasn't your energy that caused this situation.

In a broad sense the energy coming in always waits until it is appropriate to enter the form. It can vary by the relationship between the parents and child. There are no set rules here. Every agreement has a different time signature. In your case it was the entry of the soul that caused the difficulty.

This particular "child"/entity is one of great energy... the attraction to the two of you decided way before the conception of the linear form. In its haste to arrive in your union there was a miscalculation of vibration that the soul energy misunderstood.

The form fell away but the energy of this soul continues to hover about both of you. There will be another attempt.

This energy is bountiful in its integrity of energy. It was a little hasty in its blending. It doesn't care what you create as its label, it merely desires connection with both of you. Yes there will be a second attempt very soon. The energy is deciding how best to proceed.

You are suffering because of the misfire in connection and because you are so focused in your present there is a sense of responsibility. Understand that there will be connection--- and a dynamic being will forever change this experience for all of you.

Fear not. Next time there will be union.

Prepare yourself for intense connection for all three of you.

You won't have to wait long.

-VERONICA

14

Dear Veronica,

I am married to a wonderful man, but lately he has been getting on my nerves so bad.

I love to be happy and I love being around people who make me laugh.

My husband is hard to play and joke with, he takes EVERYTHING seriously and being with him is like being with a robot, no emotions, nothing.

Because of this I have no sex drive with him at all. It is like having sex with a pillow or something, there is no romance, no creativity, nothing. It is starting to bring me down.

I've tried everything, candles, music ideas of having a romantic picnic dinner etc... but he is always too tired to do anything.

The other side of this, is that he always interrupts me when I'm talking, tries to finish my sentences for me and insists I mean it the way he is perceiving it. It then turns into an argument.

I feel sad, like I can't be myself around him, I can't open up and be honest because he may take it wrong and usually if he doesn't like what I am saying he will blow me off or tell me he doesn't want to talk about it. Therefore there are many issues that have gone unresolved and now I feel resentment towards him and I just don't talk to him anymore.

He also is a pack rat, has more junk piled up in the garage from floor to ceiling and in our basement and just about every corner of the house. To me it reflects how he lets things build up as he procrastinates everything or pretends that things are not happening.

With all of this, I am overwhelmed and just don't know how to deal with it. I love him, but I don't like the contention and the clutter and the lack of intimacy.

Do you have any suggestions?

Lonely, desperate wife

Dear LDW,

Relationships are always a delicate balance of truth with your partner and truth with yourself.

Your opening sentence about this wonderful man certainly entertains the notion that there are redeeming qualities with this individual.

The path that you share through marriage is split over the truth. Thus each of truthful communications between the two of you has left both of you on a singular lonely venture.

Think to a time when you were more enamored with the possibilities instead of disappointments. Perhaps you thought he could change while he dreamed of your equal change of heart. Resentment is a product of hopeful vision in relationships unfulfilled.

The only thing that will save both of you is the truth. He is just as disillusioned as you are. Instead of expecting change of action, why not create a change of perspective? Each of you asking the other to alter personal perspectives of something that irks both of you about the other.

One thing. Not so much when there is so much there that is overlooked through ego and anger.

Go to the place in time when you felt the first pangs of attraction then recreate the scenarios that brought you together to begin with.

The rest is all linear drama.

--VERONICA

Editor's note: The above letter to DEAR VERONICA was edited for length but not for content, and also to remove some personally identifying information.

15

Dear VERONICA,

I've recently found my birth family and am totally in love with them. They would love for me to move to their state, two days away, which means my leaving a good job and my daughter and granddaughter.

I'm in a quandary because I do love my job but my health is not strong. Fibromyalgia weakens me even though I try to ignore to cope with it.

Any suggestions or ideas I can think about to help guide me into a positive experience?

Be Peace, Mary Teresa

Dear Mary Teresa,

Fibromyalgia is a disease that is a result of non-movement within the physical. The movement can be defined many ways. We suggest less sugar and salt in the diet along with exercise of any sort that is available to you. A mild stretching of muscles will relieve the discomfort you feel. Attempt as much movement as you can.

As for your family we understand your need for connection. It has been a sore spot for you for many years. Now that you have reunited there is great desire to continue the connection.

We will, however, give you this.

The granddaughter has great need of your energy. If you leave her physically she will feel the same pull of energy that you have always felt.

She needs your energy to become who she fully intends to be.

Perhaps a compromise of sorts is needed here. Withdrawing fully from your own path will not fulfill you. Spend your rest moments with your birth family ----- extend stays where needed.

Your grand baby has need of you. Keep that in mind when you make the decision. She incarnated to be in your realm of existence.

Honor that.

-VERONICA

Editor's Note: Since VERONICA is saying what she "sees" regarding a physical condition, please take particular note of the disclaimer language, which appears in virtually every issue of "Inner Whispers". What VERONICA says is NEVER intended to be medical advice. VERONICA is a nonphysical entity stating what she sees in the moment. That's all. Since you are physical, if you seek medical advice, talk to a doctor or other licensed medical professional VERONICA's words are offered only as a perspective and a non-professional observation to think about or to discuss with a licensed medical professional.

16

Dear VERONICA,

If one wants to stop the cycle of re-incarnation then is it in one's own hands not to come back or are you forced to come back no matter what or if you have to come back? Can you request not to come back?

My guru has mentioned that if you practice meditation daily then you will have a choice whether to come back or not.

You could get absorbed into universal consciousness if you are truthful in your spiritual practice.

Please advice from your perspective.

Thanks.

--Deepak

Dear Deepak,

Reincarnation is an opportunity to evolve. There is always choice involved.

Meditation is a great tool to enable the consciousness to focus, however, it is all about the lessons your eternal entity wishes to experience.

For you the choice is always available. If you have satisfaction on an eternal level you most likely will abdicate further incarnations.

The end result will always include completion of the lessons you have chosen for yourself.

-VERONICA

17

Dear VERONICA,

I lost the biggest part of my life... my dog... Ali, only 3 years old, due to my irresponsibility.

How do I come to terms with the guilt, trauma, loss, immobilizing pain of losing my Beautiful Ali??

How can I redeem myself? How can I communicate with her?

How do I get answers??

Thank you,

Shellie

Dear Shellie,

By recognizing the relationship and its lessons one can come to terms with guilt, trauma & immobilizing pain of perceived loss.

Ali knows you well and continues to be present whether in your current state you realize it or not.

By taking upon yourself the loss you are missing the lesson. Pay attention to the choice making moments of your life. We venture to say that by doing so the mistakes of your past will dim in the future choices in your life that will be forever shaded by this event.

Ali will return perhaps with more lessons mainly because there is a representation of one of your guides within her.

Redeem your self by focusing on encountering her. She is certainly focused on it. Perhaps by dual thought the reunion will be sooner rather than later. Look for her, she will arrive just when you have despaired of ever seeing her again. She cannot resist you.

She seeks reunion swiftly.

Open your mind to that instead of focusing on the loss.

Love never ends ------ it continues ------- as will the two of yours.

Open your eyes.

    -VERONICA

18

Dear VERONICA,

I have really come to enjoy reading the things that you have had to say since I subscribed to your newsletter.

Thank you for your interesting commentary, and valuable thoughts on ideas for life and working with life. I do have a question about this time period, and people who take advantage.

I am a person who has studied with Seth and Jane Roberts, and Seth has said that no one can be hurt, really, and those doing harm will hurt themselves.

It seems though, that we have some people who are lurking in our lives who do cause harm; to us and to others. In fact I have wondered if I should unsubscribe to your newsletter, because I do not want those people focusing in on you and your household.

They seem very able to try to influence anyone they cast their eyes upon in what I see as a negative way- rather than wanting to use the positives of the universe, which is what my husband and I are interested in.

Do you have any perspective upon this that you feel like mentioning?

I have really appreciated you and your viewpoint a number of times now.

Thank you.

Best Wishes to you, and Light sent to you,

LL

Dear LL,

From our perspective the core of energy expands to the infinitive knowing positively of what it is and where it is wishes to expand.

Yes, negativity feels more compounded from a linear perspective, however, ultimately it always circles back to itself leading to its demise.

This demise is not an ending but a revelation that the energy involved has no place in the infinite. Thus it resolves its issues and becomes whole.

Whole in the sense of its evolution out of the darkness to the light.

The light being the goal to understanding and becoming much more, not less.

More in the fact of resonating with the whole essence of energy, not negating its progress.

The battle you witness is only filled with fear from a limited linear perspective.

We are infinite and embrace it ----- you are on the path, be not distracted by the supposed evil ones.

In the infinite they do not exist because there you do not give them energy.

By depriving those negative ones of your energy they will ultimately have no place to go but back to themselves.

To themselves they will reconstruct the path they seek; ultimately evolving.

We are not afraid nor should you be.

-VERONICA

19

Dear VERONICA,

What does the role of severe depression play in a soul's personal development in this incarnation?

-Violet

Dear Violet,

Depression participates as an impediment to the development of the soul: Each experience highly stylized for the particular individual. It serves as judgment for the ego's mind's eye of where the soul's evolution should be. When the linear moment within the life feels inadequate or non-successful the ego steps in to create a status of environment that freezes the development of the mind's eye of the soul.

Sometimes it is necessary for the pause to occur. It offers contemplation deep within that would, and could, not occur otherwise.

Ultimately the higher self of the individual steps in to rectify the situation. It should be noted that the higher self garners the information acquired during the depression to aid in the development of the whole entity.

-VERONICA

20

Hi April,

I have been receiving your newsletter and love it. I especially love the Dear VERONICA column where you answer questions.

Dear VERONICA,

I have this burning question that I am having trouble answering. Maybe you can help me and millions of others- or refer me to someone or to material that can help.

When a person deliberately and maliciously intends harm to another what is the recourse? What happens to that unkind person?

Through my meditation, I understand that spiritual growth is tarnished, slowed down and such.

Is that correct? I am struggling with a very unkind person hurting me and she 'appears' to have gotten 'away with it'.

I appreciate your time.

Sincerely, Adele

Dear Adele,

In the whole environment of manifestation the ying and yang of experience occurs continuously. Those who participate in a negative fashion will and shall ultimately evolve to a more positive position.

The balance between good and evil exists singularly and vastly in all experiences. Each soul/entity seeks to understand all aspects of existence.

Currently this negative individual is highly involved with negative perspective. Her soul is seeking balance but is finding it hard to do so. In this life she may not be successful.

However, be assured that she will seek you out in another moment to make restitution for her negativity this time.

Send her positive energy even if you feel slighted by the encounter.

She is not getting away with anything in the big picture. It is her lack of self that propels her to act in this fashion. It continues as her thirst for connection eludes her throughout her negativity.

She suffers more than you know. You only see the illusion of the environment she has created. The balance pursues her and it is not pleasant.

-VERONICA

21

Dear Veronica,

Can you help me to better understand how a soul chooses it's time to return to spirit?

My dear, beloved husband passed over three years ago. It was a second marriage. One in which we both grew enormously. We were very much in love and were looking forward to many more years together after many years of trouble and sadness for each of us.

Does a personality/ego ever dissuade a soul from leaving? Is this leaving preordained? I've read so much yet I still can't fully accept that this beloved person would choose to leave.

Yet when I saw a medium he told her his "options were up". Really? Did he have earlier options that he was able to extend for some reason? Can you help me fully understand this part of our life?   *--Dawn*

Dear Dawn,

The movement from life to life is a chosen moment. There is nothing pre-ordained as you state it. The constant choice of the soul is always available. There are life plans that may or may not come to fruition according to the choice process of the soul that inhabits the body.

The variables in a universal perception are vast and not easily answered in this forum. We will tell you that lessons learned by the absence of a lover can be more powerful than the lessons in its presence.

When you encounter him again the attraction will be more powerful than the preceding moments.

You will see him again.

-VERONICA

22

Dear Veronica,

We adopted a precious pit bull puppy about thirteen years ago. He was a wonderful dog and everyone who knew him adored him. He recently died of what we think was just old age. He didn't like being alone, he was quite sociable. We are heart broken and want to know if he is with either mine or my husband's family on the other side and if he knew we were trying to help him by giving him medicine.

Also, he was quite large and striking, white with a brindle right eye and ear. Since his death, there has been a large white bird with dark markings that comes to our house and flies over, sits in the tree, sits on the fence and chirps, and I wonder if it could be a sign from him.

We've never seen a bird like this before and we've always had a busy bird feeder. I did get a good photograph of him. -Karen

Dear Karen,

The dog is neither with your husband's family nor your own (on the other side). He is free and taking shape close to your own family.

Since he felt such closeness to both of you he decided to keep his energy close. The bird was an easy mark and coincided with the freedom he sought from a malfunctioning body that no longer served him. He remembered a moment of envy when he saw birds flying by and sought to have the experience for himself.

He seeks another body that will make its way to you. That is why he chose a bird, to be able to see all opportunity. He is your buddy and wishes to stay with you. Seek a moment where you will let a newer version of himself to you.

He awaits the opportunity. He is not finished being with you! He will fly until the moment serves him. He knew quite well how much you loved him. You did not want him to go and he knew it.

He will return to you.

Be watchful.

-VERONICA

Editor's Note: Pets, particularly dogs and cats can "blend" with other pets and even wild animals to hang around or visit after they "die". They also reincarnate and return to the same family more often then most people might suppose. Some of April's clients have had remarkable experiences with this... as have we.

23

Dear VERONICA,

What is the origin of ignorance in the human mind? Why were we created simple and ignorant? As ignorance is very much a part of much of our human suffering it would be nice to know where that ignorance came from and the purpose of our ignorance and suffering.

Sincerely,

Bill

Dear Bill,

The ignorance you describe is merely the intense focus of the soul as it participates in a linear way. Younger souls feel the need to fully engage in the physical often losing all eternal knowledge in the process. The loss is not permanent; however, it often requires many experiences or lifetimes to align the soul knowledge with the physical engagement.

The suffering that you infer comes from the "disconnect" felt by the eternal self as it moves through physical incarnation to evolvement.

Of course it is not necessary but the young soul often does not comprehend the availability to participate at both levels.

As for yourself, the idea of separation feels idiotic and completely unnecessary. That is because of your more advanced soul level and experience.

If you seek what your contribution would be to an ignorant world, begin by living as an example to those still trapped, or on the precipice of becoming wise.

It is your best contribution. There are those who will follow at best and mimic at worst, but there can be growth.

-VERONICA

24

DEAR VERONICA,

ON APRIL 2, ON THIS YEAR I LOST MY DAD. THEY SAID HE HAD A HEART ATTACK AND PAST IN HIS SLEEP. HE WAS 54 YEARS OLD.

I HAD NOT SEEN OR TALKED TO MY DAD IN SEVERAL YEARS DUE TO DIFFERENCES IN LIFE STYLES. I LOVED MY DAD VERY MUCH AND I, AM, WITH A LOT OF GRIEF AND "SHOULD HAVE DONES". I ALWAYS THOUGHT THAT WE WOULD HAVE A CHANCE TO "FIX" WHAT WAS GOING ON BETWEEN US.

GROWING UP MY DAD WAS THE GREATEST. I COULD NOT ASK FOR ANYTHING ANY BETTER. ONCE I WAS MARRIED WE KIND OF DRIFTED APART.

HE USED TO SAY THAT I WAS GROWN AND DIDN'T NEED HIM ANY MORE, TRUTH IS I STILL NEED HIM. I

WAS ALWAYS A "DADDY'S" GIRL AND WHEN THINGS CHANGED BETWEEN US IT WAS A REALLY HARD THING FOR ME.

AS TIME WENT BY I LEARNED TO DEAL WITH IT AND FOUND A PLACE TO. I THOUGHT! WHEN HE PASSED AWAY I WAS LEFT WITH YEARS OF UNANSWERED QUESTIONS AND STILL WANTING MY DADDY!

I NEVER GOT A CHANCE TO TELL HIM HOW MUCH I LOVED HIM AND THAT NOTHING HE DID EVER CHANGED THAT. I WANTED TO KNOW IF HE IS OK AND IF HE IS AROUND ME AND IF SO DOES HE TRY TO SHOW ME OR TELL ME THINGS. THANKS FOR YOUR TIME AND HELP.

SINCERELY,

MISSY K

Dear Missy K,

Your father while physical always felt left behind by you. Once in spirit he recognized that it was only your need to be independent. He is still about you. He knows your love, it is only your regret that impedes your connection to him.

He is at your side and will be the first to help you when you embrace transition (death).

He is more than OK. He is always attempting to give you signs of his continuance. Be more observant, the signs are obvious.

-VERONICA

25

Dear VERONICA,

My name is October & I would like to ask you a question about something that has been happening to me for the past 5 years or so.

Whenever something bad or is going to happen to myself, immediate family, & or soul friend, an odd thing occurs. I get the feeling of static electricity & a feeling of someone running their fingers through my hair & scalp.

I also feel a static electricity current running down the left side of my head & body. It only happens on my left side.

I am extremely curious about this phenomena & so far no one has been able to provide an explanation for it. This phenomena has warned me a countless number of times that something unpleasant, dangerous, or bad is going to occur. I never know what the event will be - only that it is negative.

Thank you so much for your help.

Bright Blessings!

October

Dear October,

It is a deeply felt energy source that your higher self has created to enable your present manifestation to evolve more fully.

It is a gift to you from yourself.   Look not upon it negatively.   Your zeal for evolvement transcends it all.   Feel blessed by the experience. Use it wisely.

--VERONICA

26

Dear VERONICA,

How do I go about connecting with the partner that recently passed? We were with each other for 16 years and I feel as if a part of me is missing. I have wanted so much to get some kind of message from him either through my dreams or through someone else but have gotten nothing. His ex-girlfriend from High School had a dream where he is concerned about her well being and I can't say how sad that has made me feel because I wonder why he has not done the same for me. He was so much the life line of our family and now it is all gone. I hope that you can help me. Sincerely, Marie

Dear Marie,

Your disappointment clouds the experience of the now. Simply put, the connection is more subtle than your expectations.

--VERONICA

27

Dear VERONICA,

Hello,

Two years ago this week my late husband left to go back to war. He was in the Marine Corps. We just had our 2nd son Gabriel and 20 days after he was born Zach left.

This was not the first time he had been to Iraq, it was the second. It was the fastest deployment I had ever been through it seemed.

On Jan 6 2005 I got a wake up call. I walked down my stairs to the marines in blues coming through my door. I knew something had happen. I was told sorry and that is all I remember for the most part.

He was my love no matter what. We always told each other 1000 times over how much we loved each other and always to infinity and beyond we would say.

I sat in the rain for days, I lit candles. I waited and I waited. I just wanted a notion that he was there. We had been married 4 years that week. To be so close I don't get it. I'm so open and wanted him to come to me and say he was okay and two years later not a thing, no dream, nothing.

I don't understand it. Why?

Does he know that he is gone? And why won't he come to me? Everyone else seems to have seen him but I'm the closest one to him and nothing.

Please help. Will I ever get that I'm okay you're doing great with the boys with out me?

--Anonymous

Dear Anonymous,

In this instance your husband is still at war. He writes letters but feels guilt for his absence from his family. Upon resolution of this there will be contact.

--VERONICA

(Editor's note: VERONICA is speaking about her husband's current state of mind in the Afterlife here and is saying that once he resolves his issues, there will be contact.)

28

Dear VERONICA,

Last year I experienced something so beautiful that I did not even know was possible. Since then I have wanted to get back there and channel again but am struggling to do so. I have been trying to find my balance and I hope that I am on my way there. Do you have any advice for me?

Thank you for your time.

Sincerely,

Alicia

Dear Alicia,

    The first experience had no prior experience to place a judgment upon. The moment occurred in a more spontaneous fashion.

We would suggest releasing yourself from a preconceived notion and just be.

Align it with the experience of a young child who tastes ice cream for the first time. In linear it is a sublime moment. By leaving behind expectation and just being in the moment, linear experience can occur with no boundaries.

Your are in your own way, waiting for an exact re-occurrence. Perhaps the next one is beyond what you expect.

--VERONICA

29

Dear VERONICA,

Many times I have been asked how can we know what information we are being given is true and correct particularly with trance as there is a great misconception about the procedure.

However, because I was privileged to work alongside known trance teachers and guides in the UK, I am actually unsure how to answer that question for others when they are searching the Internet for a trance service such as yours.

Therefore, I would like to ask how a person could decide before ordering a service such as yours and what to look out for?

Julie

Dear Julie,

All information given in a trance manner may not be as clear as one would like. The way to differentiate is to keep an open mind while participating. No entity will rob you of your choice making while incarnate.

The intersection of energy is more about provoking the thought process of the one who listens rather than directing it.

It should be a discussion of truth, a ponderance of the information that allows the listener to formulate his/her own decision making process. It should be information not directed or decided upon for the incarnate individual.

Life is about choice. Spirit would never make the choice for you.

--VERONICA

Editor's Note: The letter from Julie above has been edited for length but without any change to the questions or statements made.

30

Dear VERONICA,

For many years I have had the desire to work with children. I have in the past worked with dying patients and am very comfortable with death and dying.

I am a spiritual person and now want to put all my experiences to use and work with the terminally ill children and their near death experiences. I am now doing research on this subject and realize that children have a great need to be able to talk to someone about their experience, and it isn't usually possible to talk to their parents who are at the time going through their own personal hell.

I think that a good way to do this is for my miniature collie and I to work with the organization (Pet Partners). I am at a time in my life disabled and not able to work full time but am able to volunteer my time to helping others. I feel that because this decision feels so right it was meant to be.

I want my life to mean something. I want to know that this time around I did something positive and my life was not a waste.

I am hoping that you can give me some kind of guidance regarding my decision.

Thanking You

Cassandra

Dear Cassandra,

Your idea is a sound one. Children are not afraid of death. The regret is the pain they see their parents and loved ones go through.

We see a surprising response to you from these children as they recount their approach to it.

Perhaps an essay or accounting of your experiences will be comforting to those the children leave behind.

We clearly see the energy of documentation emanating from you.

It has the potential to go beyond fulfillment for you and those who read what you have written.

-VERONICA

31

Dear VERONICA,

Hello my name is Andrea, and I would very much like to know how I can contact my own guide. Also is it possible once I am able to do this for bad forces or guides to interfere or have a bad influence? I am afraid of that thank you.

Andrea

Dear Andrea,

Your guides would never allow a negative force to intrude upon your union. You are far more protected than you realize.

Expand your thoughts to your guides, they await participation on a more overt level.

-VERONICA

32

Dear VERONICA,

You stated that pets can blend with other pets.   Can humans do that too?

Nancy

Dear Nancy,

   Nothing is impossible in spirit. However, human incarnates often create singular experiences. Channeled moments within other human forms have and do occur.

   -VERONICA

33

Dear VERONICA,

I have been having some problems with people and family around me. Half of my family is becoming Christian (not that I have a problem with that). But they know I'm a person who believes in spirits and ghosts, aura, all the things you have said in your newsletters.

Yet, they say my beliefs are lies. I'm put to a lot of pressure when they ask me about my faith in God whom, I do know is here with me always. I've shunted myself from them when we speak of life or death. I'm no longer afraid of either yet with my family, I can't even say anything like about my spirit guides (got 2) experiences because they will go ahead and say what I study is the devil.

Although I don't believe them, I feel much alive, and in the path in finding me when I'm like this. How can I live and have my respect of what I am when they will use their religious words against me, like saying that witches were the devil. I believe NOT!

And I feel they are gonna blame the devil for me having such thoughts, that's like saying I'm controlled and not being myself, things are all in a swirl.

My friends are Catholic. I feel they see me as lost. Am I really lost? I Don't think I am. What should I do? Because of all I learned I've helped so many people, am I the one who needs help? What do you think?

Lately we have been into pure fights, to avoid it is to say nothing. Thank you for your time.

--Miriam

Dear Miriam,

You are not lost. The belief in cultural religions is often a basic need of those who fear their spiritual internal energy.

Putting the god energy outside the self is necessary for those who feel unworthy. Beliefs are personal. It's futile to argue about it. Simply live your life and let them live theirs.

In the end the truth will be revealed to them, but the messenger will not be you.

-VERONICA

34

Dear VERONICA,

I am wondering if indeed one chooses his/her family? Is the individual aware of DNA?

I am wondering because of terminal genetic diseases. Are there random accidents or disease that the individual is unaware of? I have lost friends and family due to both and have always thought about these questions. I would appreciate any insight that could be shed on this subject!

Thank you for your time and consideration on this matter.

Sincerely, Jere

Dear Jere,

Yes the soul is quite aware of DNA when incarnating.

Past life experience sometimes needs clarification by inhaling a genetic difficulty in the current moment.

Most all those who incarnate at some point choose to experience terminal illness or discomfort.

It gives the soul much clarity and balances personal opinion on an eternal level.

-VERONICA

35

Dear VERONICA,

With the Mayan calendar and earth cleansing coming, along with the dark agendas goals seemingly happening, what purpose is there these days in the human physical world? I've lost so much inspiration for life. It is getting hard to keep my sanity.

Debi

Dear Debi,

When there is heightened focus in the linear the omnipotence of the eternal feels unattainable. Any calendar may prohibit energy through concentrated thought based in linear.

Remember who you are and the multiple linear moments you have participated in. This seemingly turbulent time frame is actually a condensed opportunity for evolvement. Growth is not comfortable. It is a stretching of one's experience, often accompanied by perceptions of misaligned agendas. Do not become distracted by the current surroundings.

Reality is created by one thought at a time. Perceive thought eternally not in a linear fashion.

-VERONICA

36

Dear VERONICA,

Veronica, could you please tell me the name of my spirit guide. I try to talk to my guide but I don't know what I'm doing wrong?

Thanks, Ruth

Dear Ruth,

Contact with a spirit guide is a highly personal non-linear event. Words are usually inadequate. Think about "being with" the energy that surrounds you rather than identification with labels.

-VERONICA

37

Dear VERONICA,

I have been practicing my many gifts and finding new ones along the way of my journey. My question is, people often ask me what my path is and I don't know how to reply. I do not label myself as anything. I have been often called an intuitive, a gate keeper, a protector, and a mystical walker.

What I am? I am really confused by all this labeling. I believe in many things. Am I going down the right path in my pursuit of becoming more spiritual?

Thank you for your time and help.

    --Anonymous

Dear Anonymous,

You have one foot in the linear and the other in eternal. Let them ask. It's better to dispense with labels. They are indeed confusing and confining.

You are not fully yourself yet............ever evolving. Yes.

Pursue the eternal ---- often.

-VERONICA

38

Dear VERONICA,

Sometimes I'll be busy doing something or driving and this wave of sadness will come over me.

It could be I heard a song that reminded me of a past love, or it could be a thought of him, or a feeling of emptiness.

I read your quote on the email that the eternal moment of freedom can be mistaken for emptiness.

Would this trigger sadness in me? The man just wasn't all that important for all this grief or sadness that overtakes me. I feel confused by it.

Thank you,

Susan

Dear Susan,

The energy of a relationship is what you miss. There is a flow to it that can trigger grief at its loss. You are correct, it's not the man, it's the connection.

This can be alleviated by opening yourself to new possibilities and what they can create. We sense a highly charged give & take, so perhaps the emptiness should be "lived through" to make way for this opportunity.

Focus on the energy.

-VERONICA

39

Dear VERONICA,

What happens to pets (dogs) who are put to sleep by their owners for health reasons?

Do they have peace ? Are they in heaven (so to speak) with our other loved ones ?

Thank you... Sylvia

Dear Sylvia,

They awake to new possibilities free of the physical angst that may have hindered their perspectives while in a body that no longer served them.

Reincarnation is a high probability.

--VERONICA

40

Hello VERONICA

Can you tell us if the humans came about from the evolvement of ape (monkey)? Were humans at one time rocks, minerals, plants, animals then humans? Or, humans were put on earth as humans only from another dimensional reality?

Thanks, Deepak

Dear Deepak,

The human form evolved from a small cell of energy. Spirit decided upon a union much later. The chicken and the egg will be debated for quite a spell. Why not focus on the union and what it can do for the soul in the experience?

-VERONICA

41

Dear VERONICA,

My beloved mother passed to spirit in 2005 in my home with her family around her. She was my best friend.

She died from Alzheimer's disease and could not respond the last week of her life. I miss her so much and I don't know how to live without her. I wish for a conversation with her in my dreams that I will remember when I wake, but nothing yet. I pray every day for this. I just need to know that she is still with me because I need her more than ever. Thanks for your time. Donna

Dear Donna,

She currently experiences a life review, which is the reason you do not "feel" her as you "knew her". Be patient, her intent lies with you.

-VERONICA

42

Dear VERONICA,

My husband died 2 months ago. At his time of death in the hospital (unknown to me) a dish went flying out of my hand. Could this have been a message from him telling me he died? I would like to know he is ok, where he is, and if he is happy with the funeral arrangements I made for him.

Luvinia P.

Dear Luvinia,

He is quite well. There is apology for the flying dish. He did not know his own strength of energy. He meant to take your hand.

Fishing.

-VERONICA

43

Dear VERONICA,

I need some help here. Is it OK to ask "why" and "what am I doing wrong?" I like the current direction of my life and am wondering why money is not manifesting? Is asking that question the reason why it is not manifesting? Or am I just rushing it somehow?

Thanks so much, Martha

Dear Martha,

It is always welcomed -- the "why" -- by the universe. It is the "doing wrong" that confounds you. Eliminate the negative opinion and see what happens.

-VERONICA

44

Dear VERONICA,

What happens to the soul during and after a suicide? This does not seem like the "Natural" time to leave the physical existence. Thank you. L. C.

Dear LC,

Each experience is individualistic. The problems and or feelings they wish to leave behind will only follow them to another life.

Upon a suicidal death the soul is usually greeted by guides and loved ones who will aid them in their process to resolve what led them to end their physical in such a way.

There is no judgment.

-VERONICA

Dear VERONICA,

I commend you for reaching out to people that may need some help and can't afford to get any answers. So hats off to you.

I have had an issue that has been affecting me for a long time, years actually. I dated a boy years ago. His name was Saul a lovely young man and he was killed on purpose.

I have dreams about him and I know that there's something he is trying to tell me but I don't get it. I was very young and don't think that I have ever come to peace with it. I'm very spiritual and I can't figure out what he is trying to tell me.

I had a reading 7 years ago and he came through by someone who is very good but all I was told is that he is watching out after me and that I'm supposed to do something that we were going to do.

It bothers me so much and I need some answers to get passed it.   If you could help me I would certainly appreciate it very much.

Thank you, Caryn

Dear Caryn,

He wishes you to find happiness, which is what you would have achieved with him. His energy can still blend with yours and he will make it available.

"Be Happy" is the message.

-VERONICA

45

Dear VERONICA,

I have two wonderful little boys, age 3.5 and 2. I would really like to teach them, or rather enable them, to keep their close connection to spirit that all children have but often lose to the physical realities of life on earth.

Do you have advice for me and other mothers who want to make sure their children keep that close connection? Or, is it our job to do that? Perhaps each child has to make that decision for themselves?

Love,

Sheryl

Dear Sheryl,

Memories of spirit often fade as the harsh realities of physical present themselves. Often children continue to feel and see the presence of their guides long after they stop talking about them. Some parents aid the process [of forgetting] by not encouraging the children to talk about what they see, feel, and hear.

The two gentle souls who are your sons chose you in particular for a mother in hopes that you would keep their connection alive in their consciousness. They have a spiritual agenda that will reveal itself when they are older.

   -VERONICA

46

Dear VERONICA,

I was wondering if you would by any chance know about the meeting of my soulmate? I do know with my strong intuition that he will be coming into my life at any moment now, and it is exciting to me as I know that our divine love will be phenomenal. I also feel that he may well be my Twin Flame soulmate. Can you please send me a line or two about our meeting? I would really appreciate it with all love.

Blessings, ~Crystal~

Dear Crystal,

The meeting will happen when you are fully engaged in your Spiritual energy. Live each day fully with joy. This abundance of energy will attract exactly what you seek.

A vortex approaches you. Ready yourself. Like attracts like always. You are ready. It most likely will occur when you least expect it.

The details are of your own thoughts. Daydream about it and see what occurs. Your creation will be to your specifications, so be clear.

-VERONICA

47

Dear VERONICA,

Your newsletters have been so insightful. Thank you very much for sharing your knowledge!

I have a question regarding my husband, Jeff. He was born in 1968 and has not ever been in the military, however, he is sure he fought and died in Vietnam.

He has memories and details of being there and his company of fellow soldiers. I believe him. However, he needs some kind of closure to move forward or something because this is really holding him back.

Plus, it affects me and our children because he sometimes acts as if we are his military unit, as if he is living that life currently.

How can I help him get past this or get closure or verification? He is consumed with this issue and can't seem to move forward. He has trouble allowing himself to be successful and I wonder if his past is holding him back in the present.

Thank you.

Debbie,
Oklahoma

Dear Debbie,

You are correct in your assumptions; however, the complexity of the past life upon your husband is intense.

A series of regressions may help to resolve the incompleteness he experiences from that time. He carries guilt about what occurred in that time.

-VERONICA

48

Dear VERONICA,

All the great masters tell us that the spirit of god is within us. This spirit is god dwelling within us. My question is why do we not listen to this spirit within us and practice love and intelligence rather than what we often practice, which is hate and ignorance?

Bill

Dear Bill,

There are many reasons for not listening. Most involve dramas created by those who do not have the inner wisdom at their disposal. They are dominated by the lure of it.

-VERONICA

49

Dear Veronica,

My husband Dennis was in an accident at work in September of 1999 and has suffered injuries in his back where he has severe muscle spasms. He was a carpenter by trade but has not been able to go back to work since the accident. Can he heal his physical body through meditation, and if so what would you suggest?

Grateful for your advice.

Debera

Dear Debera,

Yes he can.

It would require clear focus and a fluid thought process.

-VERONICA

50

Dear VERONICA,

I'm a 34 year old woman with children ages 14 and 11. After 14 years of marriage I left my husband as we stopped being a couple and lived separate lives for 3-4 years ago. My ex wanted his cake and wanted to eat it too, so he became quite mean and selfish when I left.

He told my son some very bad things about me and now my son doesn't want to see me as his dad would not allow it anyway. He is also selfish and doesn't want to give me what I deserve from settlement, so we are forever going to court.

Do you see my son coming with me and what the outcome would be with settlement, and will I ever find happiness again?

Thank you

Worried Virgo

Dear "Worried",

By involving yourself in this drama you may not see the path clearly.

The outcomes depend on how positive you remain. It's always dark before a storm but once the winds die down, the rain cleans the air. Be the one to welcome the rain. You will pass through these difficult times.

Happiness will be yours, but not exactly the way you envision it at the moment. Keep your thoughts positive.

-VERONICA

51

Dear VERONICA,

My name is Wesley and I have a few things that are weighing very heavy on my mind. I am 38 years old and I had a brother who was 36 years old but he died Oct. 22.

He was found dead in bed. I really need to ask a question about life after death. Three days after my brother's death my daughter had a baby girl. Her name is Caroline. She was born premature.

I was wondering if it's possible that my brother's spirit or soul could have entered into the new life form?

I know it sounds crazy, but I have lost a lot of family lately and it seems like a new baby is born every time. For example, I was born 1968. 3 days after my mom's little brother drowned I was born and I was given his name, which is Wesley.

So would you please email me back and talk with me about this subject? It is very important to me.

Thank you very much for your time.

Wesley

Dear Wesley,

You are correct in your thoughts, however, it is more complex than this.

--VERONICA

52

Dear VERONICA,

I have been on my spiritual path now for 3 yrs. I started off in a mental circle looking for answers after losing my 18 yr old son in a car crash. It gave me peace and strength just being there.

After a few months trance started with me. I then moved on to a trance circle where it became obvious that my path was transfiguration. I have been having problems with the voice box. I go into light trance, feel my guide with me, feel the cold air that surrounds me, but when our medium asks for my guide to speak nothing happens. I think I may have blocked myself in the mental circle because the medium there knew nothing about trance.

I used to stop myself going into trance. We had a transfiguration demonstration by our medium in which my son came through and it was wonderful. My guide also came through and asked me why am I not speaking in trance. I said I am trying very hard, but nothing seems to be happening. He said go forward with my trance and transfiguration work. I feel such a failure because of this and I really want to work for Spirit.

A few months ago just after my son's anniversary, I heard Spirit talk to me which was wonderful. Even though you know Spirit is with you, to hear them just makes you realize the wonder of it all.

If you could give me any advice on this I would be grateful.

When I meditate at home I have started to manipulate my arms and body and feel my face change and have the above changes, but I don't seem to have any response from my guide in either thoughts or pictures and I don't know what I am doing wrong.

Could you help me?

Thank You, Betty.

Dear Betty,

It is the freeness of emotion that is the missing ingredient. You have bottled up a bit after the loss. Allow your heart to be itself again. What you seek is available but it needs the emotion to proceed.

-VERONICA

53

Dear VERONICA,

My wife passed on after a prolonged stressful illness. My understanding is that it takes a period of time of rest on the other side for recovery. I pray for my wife daily and speak to her at times. I am thinking of her and tell her I love her, but I don't want to hold her back from progressing. Is she aware of my prayers and my talking and thinking of her?

Thank you, George

Dear George,

Yes. She is contemplating another experience but has decided to wait until you are with her.

--VERONICA

54

Dear VERONICA,

I am really starting to freak out. I started meditating a week ago. First of all I had reiki and it just kept flowing from there. In one week I have had two absolute strangers that have either suggested or bought crystals for me whilst saying that I hold high spiritual powers. One lady asked if I was a clairvoyant the other lady told me that my creative ability would soon be seen. I can't stop thinking about all of this. Can you please help with clarity and guidance? Please and Regards.

Theresa

Dear Theresa,

The opening to the eternal self is very personal in nature. You have created visual linear moments to tell yourself it's time to do.

Instead of freaking out, the moments would be better spent looking inward.

There is nothing fearful about connecting to your true self.

The abilities are natural. Own them and move forward. There are those who will benefit from your personal reunion.

    --VERONICA

55

Dear VERONICA,

I have some complicated series of questions on the nature of reality. Later questions depend on answers to the former. The first is to simply confirm, from your knowing, as to whether there really are alternate realities of each of our lives.

Are there new realities created for each decision we face? Is there a threshold to make that split? Obviously, with billions of people making decisions everyday, there would be an infinite number of realities that exist.

So this would pose a very complicated scenario of transition into the next life when taking all those realities into consideration.

Regards,

Steve

Dear Steve,

You are attempting analysis from linear perspective.

Outside of this reality the basis for reality isn't confined by a timeline, thus the basis to hypothesize alternate realities becomes distorted.

-VERONICA

56

Dear Veronica,

As I understand it, our soul leaves our physical body every night while we sleep to remember itself, to experience it's true essence, and re-enters the physical prior to our awakening. Is this the same as astral travel? Can you please elaborate on this?

Sincere thanks,

Catharine

Dear Catharine,

Yes, it is very similar, however, the experience is somewhat unconscious in most individuals. This has to do with the experience and intent of the soul participating.

-VERONICA

57

Dear VERONICA,

I have had the same boyfriend for 4 years and who I love very much. He has always told me he loves me more than I know and at times he's shown it. Then there's these other times when it seems like he really doesn't, because I feel at times there is no way he could let these things happen or do what he does if he really loved me the way he claims to. I really don't know if he really knows how faithful I am to him or how much I really do love him. I just want him to understand and know these things, but no matter what or how I prove them to him he still seems to forget or over look them. I don't know in my heart that he loves me at all or not. Help? Please, what do I do to save this relationship? Amy L.

Dear Amy,

Relationships should not have to be saved!

-VERONICA

58

Dear VERONICA,

I have been receiving your "Inner Whispers" for some time now and can't believe how it follows my life at times. Recently I have been over come with lonesomeness.

All I seem to have is work. I was once told by a palm reader that I would be married 3 times. I have been, but I cannot accept that there will never be any one else in my life.

I have made some bad choices in relationships and I have so much to give to some one else. Is there a chance for me? Is there something I can do?

I appreciate any words you may have

Kathy

Dear Kathy,

It is important to understand the vast possibilities within your realm of existence. Perhaps you are stuck on the suggestion of only 3 marriages.

Events are not set in stone and as the designer of your life there is always probability of creating exactly what you want.

Decide that it's time to have an appropriate person in your life   Be specific as your thoughts and ideas will follow your design. Yes there is much more my dear.

--VERONICA

59

Dear Veronica,

Hello to you and thanks for your commitment to the people on this plane. I am sending an e-mail with the romantic side of my life in question.

I'm a divorcee and have one child. I have been single now for 5 years or so and would like to meet a partner, as I feel I'm ready now. I would appreciate any information you may have in regards to this. Respectfully, Lisa

Dear Lisa,

Make a list of what you would want in a partner. Be specific. Be truthful. Dedicate your thoughts positively on your list.

You might be pleasantly approached by exactly what you have written.

-VERONICA

60

Dear VERONICA,

Good Afternoon. I receive your news letters once a week. I would like to ask you a question.

My mom passed away on Oct. 3rd of this year. I miss her more now than I have in recent years. She suffered most of her life with depression and in her later life suffered with Alzheimer's.

Does it make sense that I miss her more now that she is whole emotionally and no longer suffering? I know I can not see her but feel she is around me. How will I know she is there?

My mom also named me Faith Hope at Birth. Why such a hard name to live up to, is there a purpose for this name?

Thank you for any help in advance. Reading your spiritual readings help me in my daily life to understand why we are here...we are continually learning.

Regards, Faith Hope

Dear Faith Hope,

Your mother signals all the time. Watch your surroundings closely. You will see her love and gratefulness for your continued love during this past physical.

She is no longer confused. She named you thusly because that is what you represented to her. It was more of a name for her to live up to.

In later years she felt she failed miserably. You have always represented hope to her even if she never told you.

-VERONICA

61

Dear VERONICA,

I am overwhelmingly in love with an Indian Spirit guide. His name is "Naiche". When I first saw his face on the Internet, I fell under his spell and he is now in my blood.

I cannot live this life without him. I cry knowing I cannot hold him or feel his beautiful Apache skin. He passed in 1921. What is this connection?

Love Andrea

Dear Andrea,

Several past lives including one in the late 1800's. There was great passion interrupted by circumstance. There will be reunion in the next life.

-VERONICA

62

Dear VERONICA,

I was recently taken by surprise when a man came into my life. I was not expecting it. I have had trouble adjusting and do not know where this is going. I care very much for him and have been friends with him for several years. Any advice will help.

Elaine

Dear Elaine,

The best experiences in linear are often not planned. Enjoy the spontaneity of energy. It will go on its own.

-VERONICA

63

Dear VERONICA,

My boyfriend of almost three years tragically died in a four wheeling accident. There were many unresolved issues with us. He was supposed to come to my house that night but unfortunately did not make it.

I wanted to know if his passing was quick or was he alive for sometime before actually going. Does he know how much I love him and think about him everyday? And if he comes to me, I have been trying so hard to feel his presence at home as well as at the cemetery. Is he ok with the death?

I am in deep depression thinking that he is not ok with dying and just want to know that he is ok.

Thank you,

Holly

Dear Holly,

He is contemplating his experience having been knocked out of his physical body abruptly. There was no pain, no time for fear. Suddenly he was out of body looking down on his familiar form and realized he was allegedly dead. He did not feel so.

His first thoughts were of you. He waits for you and will be there at your crossing. Death was different than his expectations. He feels clarity in his love for you and understands your connection from his new point of view. Your love is a constant for him.

-VERONICA

64

Dear VERONICA,

I have been seeing spirits for as long as I can remember. The thing is, I want to be able to communicate with them, but I don't know how.

My mother who is 94 years old is in the hospital with heart problems. When I was on my way out in my car at night I thought there was a car with high beams on behind me. When I looked in my mirror there was no car but the face of my father.

My father died awhile ago.

It looked like he wanted to say something to me, but I didn't know how. I tried to talk to him but I got nothing. Is there anything you can recommend?

MN

Dear MN,

You are seeking verbal connection. Often those in spirit communicate better through sensing.

Allow yourself quiet moments to better connect through the heart chakra. It won't be what you are expecting.

-VERONICA

65

Dear VERONICA,

I have recently come out of a long illness. I do believe that had something in me not changed, I was surely on a down hill slide and headed for an early grave. I did not want to live anymore because my quality of life was very poor.

Since that time I realized I make my own reality. This has given me power to believe anything is possible, even my own healing. My health has improved so very much and I am happy for the first time in many years. All of this has made me think of the things I loved and want in my life.

While talking with a friend I told her I wanted my precious poodle Nenna back because...after all, if all were possible...why couldn't she come back to me? I began immediately to believe then that she was coming home. I pulled out pictures and put them up at work and home and started being grateful that she was returning to me.

Losing this animal was so very devastating to me and I have never recovered from it. I felt the need when she was 13 years of age to have her put to sleep. I agonized over doing this...I did not want to do it and 12 years later tears still come to my eyes every single time I think of that day at the vet's office.

I pray she has forgiven me. It was after all this that I discovered your website and started receiving your newsletter. The very first newsletter spoke of this very situation and it validated the possibility of my desire to have Nenna return to me.

I was elated. It was no longer just a vision for me, but a blatant desire...probably one of the biggest desires I've ever had.

Can you tell me if she wants to return and if she will return to me? I love her with everything that I am. Tears always come to my eyes when I think of her; I'm crying as I write this.

She has always meant more to me than any animal I've ever had. Tell her for me how much I love and miss her.

Please help me.

Marcy

Dear Marcy,

She seeks reunion, however, the proper vehicle has not presented itself yet. Close your eyes, visualize her energy, create a bridge of love for her to cross.

Your embrace is her idea of heaven.

-VERONICA

66

Dear VERONICA,

I especially enjoyed the writings on transition. I have several people who I read to. It is such a comfort.

Whether or not it is really like this, is immaterial. It makes many people feel so much better. Well done.

Janice

Dear Janice,

Ah.... But it is.

-VERONICA

67

Dear VERONICA,

Your wisdom is so helpful. I need some clarification however, regarding being loving, caring and helpful. What about when you start feeling like you're being a "doormat" or used?

I have nicely said "no" occasionally, but then I feel guilty that I am not being there for someone when they need me, but I also need time for me. Can you clarify?

Thank You. Joanne

Dear Joanne,

Your energy is one of service. The support you give others has truly made a difference to many. However, to continually give takes an enormous amount of concentration in the linear.

When we "feel" your energy it has a depleted texture. It appears to have been quite a long time since you have replenished it.

The idea of giving is splendid and you are good at it, but the lesson of self nurturing needs to be explored. Assign yourself one personal moment per day where you can replenish your energy.

The moment will come where you will not be able to serve and that will be unfortunate for those who blossom with your attention.

View it as a refilling so that you will be able to give more.... An automobile cannot function without fuel. Fill yourself.

-VERONICA

68

Dear VERONICA,

I agree with what Tupac Says, "We're all born hungry."
Not blind. That's the truth.

When I was younger, my teachers knew me as the kid
who asks a million questions. The first question I
remember asking was when I was in Thailand. Before
me and my biological family came to America.

My biological mom had just gotten back from the market.
She had bought some ice and a few other things. I
asked her if I could see the ice. She didn't hesitate to
show it to me. It was a block.

I'm not sitting here, trying to find a reason for why I have
congenital glaucoma. I don't bring that topic up in all of
my writings, but it has been a wonderful experience.
Honestly, I don't think I'll ever be there. I mean blind.
This a perfect ingredient for an integrated soul. Don't you
think?

I guess the universal law, "like attracts like" can put its two cents in. After all, I am that man. It's hard for people to find a definition for the word "blind."

I'm doing fine. I get to pursue my career with animals and everything else I want and need. I guess the animals that appeared in my dreams have been taking care of me, besides myself.

Smokie

Dear Smokie,

The entity from which you evolved is not blind. The sense of knowing has no idea what color is. Your life is enriched beyond the images of the ego. Your inner universe is far more complex including the images of your mind's ego.

Enjoy the experience, it will be useful in future lives where the "image of life" will have a great profound moment for you.

-VERONICA

69

Dear VERONICA ~

I have been thinking about the greatest mystery in the world, " Death", and I've been wondering why God would want to reveal this great secret and the fact that there is no death and that there is an afterlife.

I'm not sure how to express myself, but what would the world be like if everyone knew for sure and without a doubt that there is no death? How would that effect our lives and the world?   There would no longer be that divine mystery, Then What?!!!   ~ Judy ~

Dear Judy,

Then... The dogmas and fears placed upon those in physical would no longer be relevant. The infinite perspective may alter forever the negativity of your existence and place the focus divinely upon evolving.

-VERONICA

70

Dear VERONICA,

WHAT HAPPENS TO THE SOUL DURING AND AFTER A SUICIDE? THIS DOES NOT SEEM LIKE THE "NATURAL" TIME TO LEAVE THE PHYSICAL EXISTENCE.

THANK YOU, L.C.

Dear L.C.

There is great despair within the soul when there is a choice to end a life prematurely. Often linear circumstances compound upon themselves leaving the energy or soul overwhelmed.

Most find that suicide is not a solution after they are not physical because the situations and dramas follow the soul into the afterlife.

Issues are meant to be resolved while linear. Leaving physical by one's own hand does not provide a resolution, only a postponement.

All life issues are resolved while in the life. Ending the life does not mean there is finality.

It is the intent of every soul to resolve and learn. You will only reincarnate with the same dramas until you resolve it. It is not an escape.

It should be noted that there is no judgment, only continuance until the moment is given again. In other words there are no free passes out of linear.

-VERONICA

Editor's note: Some of you may recognize this question because it was answered earlier. The way that happened was that I had a scheduled meeting with VERONICA to write the Message From VERONICA column for an issue of "Inner Whispers".

I grabbed some Dear VERONICA emails in case there was some time left after the article. There was, and this was one of the letters I happened to grab.

Note that this time VERONICA wrote a much longer comment. I thought you would find it interesting. The message is the same as the earlier comment, but, in this case it is more detailed.

-Allen

71

Dear VERONICA,

First of all if by any chance you do answer this letter, I want to thank you in advance. The problem is I fell in love with a bad boy and can't seem to get him out of my system.

He has moved in with another girl and won't communicate with me even as a friend anymore.

I need to know if he will ever contact me again, even as just a friend?

I have nobody in my life at this time and I am praying for TRUE LOVE.

Thanks

Peggy

Dear Peggy,

By holding onto the hope of reconnection you are closing yourself off from other energies. True love is defined by the even exchange of energy.

It would be a more positive path to leave behind you this man. Further contact may inhibit your ability to create a more harmonious relationship.

-VERONICA

72

Dear VERONICA,

Thank you for the newsletters.

My 31 year old son, Preston, killed himself last nite.

He was so handsome and bright, but totally down on himself and miserable. He'd threatened many times, but still came as a shock.

I know he knows I loved him and I know his life trauma is being lovingly cared for, but I need something from him or my guide to tell me he's okay.

What can I do? I'm sorry if this isn't the right place to ask.

Thank you for any help.

Joni

Dear Joni,

Your son is reviewing the choices he made. The love between the two of you burns brightly and in that light Preston makes his way.

His eternal self considers much, knowing at last how right you were.

Bittersweet, he moves towards another experience to resolve the self deprecation that propelled his self destructive spiral.

You will encounter him again.

-VERONICA

73

Dear VERONICA,

I have come across your site through Abraham.

I am currently a 47 year old woman. Exotic looking, highly intelligent etc. No need for that ego stuff, over it.

What is it? I am a fashion designer, highly creative talented, you name it. I have it, looks and so on, and guess what, I spend my life almost celibate.

So loyal, sensitive hard working proud, independent, and yet very optimistic, is it past life karma, that I am paying for? You know what if you say yes, it will be easier to accept than just bad luck.

Why have doors closed in my face always, no matter how hard I tried to be optimistic? VERONICA do not come back to tell me I created it, I know I did not, there is an answer you know.

Why do I feel that I have an entity of my own they MUST come through? I really want to know.

Please help, I am at a point where I have just put my hands up, I am sick of having doors slam in my face, sick of being nice, and so on, where is my guide, why does it have to be so difficulty for me to connect to the flow?

What is it that I need to do to get things right? I am so sick of struggling and fighting and fighting against the current of life, maybe and may be I do not belong here.

What is required of me? Who am I? I need help from you! You have it and I demand it now. Please respond.

Love you anyway even if you don't.

Don't publish my name please, call me Eve if you must!!!!!!!!!!!!

My Dearest "Eve",

In the larger picture of the Universe there is always a balance of energy emanating from each source of life. In your path so far there have been several negative responses from the energy that is you. In other words, indeed there have been existences where you have been less than appreciative of the gifts you have been given.

In this life a balance of perspective is occurring that in the end run will give you the balance your soul craves.

We realize that you seek solution so we advise going with the "current" however uncomfortable you may perceive it. In that surrender and acceptance will come the connection you seek.

Know that you are so much more than you can perceive in this moment. From this life you can now have a greater appreciation of connecting.

Who are you? We say that you are a highly evolved soul at the precipice of comprehending the ideal blending of all of your lives.

We hold your hand in spirit willing you to be comforted. Yes, there is an energy also hoping to speak through you. Take a breath and allow yourself to release the frustration.

This current linear life is about loss of connection but know that your eternal self is surrounded by many who love you well.

-VERONICA

74

Dear VERONICA,

I've been in a relationship for nearly 8 yrs and there has not been one year that my fiancée has not cheated with other women.

I stayed because we have a good relationship aside from his wanderings. I hoped he would come to value what we share but this year I have made up my mind to move on with out him.

I'm a little scared but don't want to live digging around to find out what he's been up to, checking his phone messages etc. anymore.

My confidence is coming back but I need some assistance.

Anuket

Dear Anuket,

All of the energy spent investigating his truthfulness or lack thereof should perhaps be focused now on your spiritual balance and security of emotion.

Despite your acceptance of your fiancé's infidelities there is a deep bruise of betrayal on your heart.

Focus now on you. Make your comfort and happiness a priority. The energy you give yourself will attract what you deserve..... someone who treasures you beyond all others.

Focus on your heart.... it is full of love waiting to unite with someone who deserves you.

Own it..... the time is now.

--VERONICA

75

Dear VERONICA,

I have a wonderful Dog named Bear. He is going on 12 years old, a delightful Golden Retriever. We are amazed he still is with us after his rough time in the Spring.

He most likely is in pain all the time yet he has a permanent smile on his face. He can hardly stand up and so can no longer go for his beloved walks. We all feel love from him and he never complains.

However, he will sleep at the front door for as long as I am away. When I arrive home it is with a great welcoming. He says "I love you" as best he can with sounds as close as he can mimic.

When the time comes, how can one best help their beloved Dog cross over?

I am not so clairvoyant to know the best realm. I do not wish to do this too early.

*What will be the perfect time --how can I possibly know?
Bear is a retired St. John's therapy Dog for Hamilton
Ontario Canada. He visited the brain injured and
schizophrenia wards, as well as a seniors home. He
loved his Job.*

*Bear is an inspiration and I am honored for him to be
loaned to us. Will I know him again?*

:-) God Bless, Sheilagh

Dear Sheilagh,

Bear is a multi-dimensional energy that is well equipped to understanding his continuance after the physical. The smile on his face is a manifestation of his knowing that his alleged crossing to the afterlife is really an exchange of the physical form that he has participated in many times.

His primary concern is how all of you will feel during the moment.

Hold him with your love.

He will return as soon as he can. However, he's not quite finished this life yet. His understanding of the process will most likely help you through your perceived loss.

Highly evolved energy..... that is Bear.

-VERONICA

76

Dear VERONICA,

Your column guides me faithfully. In my quest to manifest financial success and since my culture of origin is rather lacking in substance, I have been pursuing exotic spiritual experiences thru dating men of middle eastern persuasion, and have finally met some VERY successful men.

My question is this...is it o.k. to lie to others as long as it doesn't bother MY conscience?? I move through relationships faster than it takes to age cheap wine, and I wonder if this is superficial?

Please be my spirit guide! Thank you for your INTUITIVE INTENSIONS! MANIFEST OUR VICTORY OVER THE WEAK! Take more TIME OFF from WORKING and HEAL the UNIVERSE.

Yours truly, BEDI

Dear Bedi,

The Truth is the only path to any success you wish to manifest. It is never a positive moment to be lying to others whether it bothers your linear conscience or not.

There is damage to the soul while participating in something that is untrue.

-VERONICA

77

(Editor's note: In the following letter VERONICA decided to write her responses to the various paragraphs under each paragraph instead of all at the end. VERONICA's comments are in regular type below each italic paragraph.)

Dear VERONICA,

Hello, again everybody. I am very thankful for your weekly news-letter,(and your effort.) and I look forward to it always. I am also a fond reader of the Seth-material, I find it very impressive and giving in every way. (By the way: do you have anything to say about Seth? ...Do you know the guy?)

VERONICA: Yes we know the energy and admire his ability to merge the eternal concepts in a linear manner.

Anyway, my question tonight is this: Seth says that very few people start out in the beginning, trying to be as bad as possible. And I understand this and I believe this thoroughly. But again, I am curious... What about those few others? What about that very small group of people, who actually start out trying to be as bad as possible? What are the mechanisms involved in this, can you say anything about it, or put it into any context?

VERONICA: We would say that it is not as linear as what you state. Energy participates for the experience with intention to do well. It is the choices in the physical that lead most to stray from the first inclination.

How does this experience and behavior affect them? How do entities or souls get involved in these tracks, and where can these tracks lead?

VERONICA: Experiences compound themselves often leading good intentions off track, so to speak.

Interesting question, I think, and I will appreciate any kind of answer... So, again, thank you for your time, and if it's anything I should know, let me know...I wish you all good, and good luck with your projects.

From Roar Mikalsen. Norway

VERONICA: You're welcome!

-VERONICA

78

Dear VERONICA,

I often ask my mother, who is deceased, for guidance. If she is in spirit form does she hear me? If she re-incarnated, who hears me?

Marie

Dear Marie,

She has not chosen to reincarnate at this time. Her energy integrates with yours fully. The words attached to your need of guidance are resonating within your energy.

Do not be fearful. She is with you in ways that cannot translate to your current moment. Continue the dialogue; you will receive your answers. It is her intention to do so.

-VERONICA

79

Dear Veronica:

I have a teen age daughter who is out-of-control. During the past six months she has cut class, drunk beer, low grades, missed curfew, lied, stolen, huge cell phone bills, inappropriate use of the computer and phone, potty mouth, and her most recent offense, getting caught shoplifting. We do not know what to do. The usual consequences, grounding and losing privileges, have not worked in the past. I am looking at different schools so I can remove her from the negative peer group she is in. Please help! Mom

Dear Mom,

Your daughter feels disconnected from her source energy. In an attempt to be "noticed" she participates in the negativity of whatever she can. Realize this is a cry for attention. She seeks her guides by acting out unfavorably because she feels desperate. --VERONICA

80

Dear VERONICA,

Does the spirit of the chicken or fish, etc. leave its body just before it is slaughtered?

I've head that we who eat their flesh (I rarely do) absorb their fear vibrations. And that animal proteins are actually more harmful to our body than beneficial. Is this true?

In which case, is the best/healthiest/most spiritual diet a vegan one -- one that excludes all animal proteins?

My main concern, though, is with the inhumane conditions that animals and poultry must endure leading up to the moments before they are slaughtered. (Maybe they would actually welcome death just to get away from their miserable, though short, lives!) Thanks for your comments on this. - K

Dear K,

There are some animal energies that agree to the food chain idea. However, there are the "victims" you have spoken of. Animals have a different commitment to the linear. A human environment is conducive to the agreement we have spoken of.

If you are a "meat eater" we would highly suggest aligning yourself with the energy of positiveness that comes from energy alignment from the animals. The animal souls have a different perception of incarnation and are more able to transition when the energy is more aligned. Therefore, seek the "food chain" in a more positive way.

-VERONICA

81

Dear VERONICA,

First of all I want you know that I truly enjoy reading Veronica's weekly messages.

I have a question regarding the message on Matters of the Heart. About a year ago I retired a 10 yr abusive relationship. How do you raise your vibration level to move on to the next relationship?

Michele

El Paso TX

Dear Michele,

It is difficult in linear to separate from abusive relationships, for the consciousness has the ability to rationalize the encounter.

It is necessary to sever one's self from the abuse which often leads to feelings of emptiness.

In your particular moment we would suggest a moment of pause where you reestablish your perspective of your energy.

It has been stifled amid the circumstances and needs the opportunity to reconnect. It is highly unlikely to attract appropriate energy until you do so.

Be kind to your self and nurture your inner heart. This should be done in a singular moment. Once finished, you will be ready for a new relationship.

-VERONICA

82

Dear VERONICA,

If none of this is real, and we are only a dream.... then how are we of any value really? I just can't imagine that Source Energy needs all of this drama for its expansion?

Thank you,

Cynthia

Dear Cynthia,

Physical reality is a gift. A pristine moment created by your entity to participate in an evolutionary process. Drama is a creation of your linear self and its value escapes most of those involved in the linear.

Dramas are equally as valid and should not be dismissed out of hand. Your entity is focused on the experience whether or not you as a singular manifestation find value in it. Your entity finds all experience relevant and does not judge the drama you create to get to the end result.

All of it has value. You are seeing and judging but a small aspect of the big picture.

-VERONICA

83

Dear Veronica,

"How you experience death is linked mostly with your emotional and spiritual state at the time of death..."

I was struck by this quote in your "Inner Whispers". My dear 20 year old son passed away recently. He was being treated for leukemia but left us very suddenly due to a sepsis infection.

I agonize every day about how scary this was for him as we were not expecting it and I didn't have a chance to say all of the things I wanted to help him prepare for the next life.

He very much did not want to die and had so much he still wanted to do here. Would my son have had a difficult and scary death experience?

I had a couple of very real dreams afterward where he seemed to be hovering here and not sure what had happened. Is this real?

As a mom, I wish only to know that my son lives on in happiness.

Please help me,

A Grieving Mother

Dear Grieving,

Your son was a little surprised at the fluidity of his crossing experience. At first he was unsure that he had even achieved it, which is why he appeared slightly confused in your dream.

It was actually not a negative experience from his perspective. It was in fact quite joyous once he realized how he retained what he lived and all of his other lives. He is not finished, which was his greatest fear, being finished.

The idea of finality no longer veiled from his perspective, he dances in the light of the eternal and encompasses a feeling of joy and freedom.

He intends to dance until you arrive ..... yes he waits for you. And yes it's all real.

-VERONICA

84

Dear VERONICA,

My professional life is beginning to look up, but my personal life is very quiet. I am a single mom and my daughter is anxious for me to get married so she can get a 'new' dad.

Sandra

Dear Sandra,

Start by deciding what you want in a mate. You certainly "know" what you don't want. It is appropriate now to engage what your heart really desires.

Write it down if you need to... give it clear thought without disruption of negativity. You may be pleasantly surprised.

-VERONICA

85

Dear VERONICA,

Our world has such turmoil right now that it is always uppermost in our thoughts that it could all be destroyed - all of it.

Would there be any repercussions in the spiritual world (your existence) if earth were completely destroyed?

> *- Donna*

Dear Donna,

Our perspective would be one of support for those energies involved in such an event. The probability always exists for destruction; however, it is important to note that the probability of restoration and harmony has equal intensity.

Perhaps a focus upon the latter would be more beneficial for your world. Even a single thought can generate enough energy to regenerate a downward spiral.

What if you were that <u>one</u> energy and you decided it was a pointless endeavor? Or that your singularity was not strong enough to make a difference?

We beseech each and every one of <u>you</u> to reconsider such a thought process.

-VERONICA

86

Dear VERONICA,

How will the experience of dying in this life into another life feel and look like? Will we be a whole being in another body?

What will it feel like the moment we detach from our physical bodies? What are we going to see and will our spirit bodies be something solid and comfortable?

Thanks.

   Anonymous

Dear Anonymous,

   Each experience is unique unto the energy. The universal viewpoint is one of continuance. The details are personal.

Yes you will retain all experience; however, the experience of a single life will be the point of perspective while engaged in the physical life. In-between all information is available.

In some cases, multiple life focus becomes available, but not often.

The feelings vary from each perspective. The transition is so smooth that some do not realize it has occurred.

Each view is unique unto the individual.

"Solid" is not a word used to describe the experience; however, there is a word "comfortable" that applies.

-VERONICA

(Editor's note: The above questions actually came in two different emails from the same person. Because they are so related, I combined the questions into a single letter to VERONICA even though VERONICA responded to each of them separately. -Allen)

87

Dear VERONICA,

I had to put my beloved dog down because he was suffering. Does he hold it against me?

Herman

Dear Herman,

Animals have a different view of the life and death process. Your dog realized the longevity of its physical had reached an end.

There was no judgment. Your friend remains just that.... your friend.

He thanks you for a great experience and possibly will attempt a reunion.

-VERONICA

88

Dear VERONICA,

My husband killed himself last month and since then I have read and studied a lot about life after death.

Many say that people that commit suicide often have to reincarnate, some say many times in order to ... what I am not sure, get it right?

That is not my question, however, my question is, if he reincarnates, how can he still be watching over me?

I have had some very real signs that he is around at his service and at home but none lately. I found the signs so comforting and worry that if he reincarnates he won't be around me anymore.

Also, if he reincarnates will he be there when I die?

I am trying to keep my thoughts on positive things in my life and making my life better by trusting my emotions to guide me. I want to think about my husband but it makes me very sad when I do.

I usually turn my thoughts to something else so I don't bring myself down and get depressed. By doing this I feel I am betraying him somehow.

It is hard to think about only the good times because my thoughts almost always end up with the vision of him dead when I found him in our bedroom. Any help you can offer is greatly appreciated.

- Unsigned

Dear Unsigned,

It is important to remember that out of linear physical there is not a time line. Your husband may reincarnate, but it does not align with what your are experiencing.

He will be and is watching over your physical. The reincarnation will occur while not conflicting with what you perceive.

The vision of his death will be in your thoughts, but perhaps creating new thoughts of reunion can put them to rest.

You will see him again.

    -VERONICA

89

Dear VERONICA,

I have a problem for which I have no rational explanation.

Whenever I am in proximity to any female having labor pains or any problem related to pregnancy, I become extremely nauseous. I do not have to be aware of the presence of the person. Once, while I was traveling I felt these familiar "symptoms". I did not know what was going on.

Then I saw the ambulance. Later, I found out that a lady was having a baby in the ambulance. There was another situation when I suffered a blackout.

This happened when a student of mine was describing her post abortion difficulties. As I attempted to walk away to get some water, I collapsed. There are countless other instances. I am now sixty-two. This has been going on for over fifty years. What's happening here?

My only explanation is that in one of my previous incarnations, I was a woman who died while giving birth to a child. Is this the correct explanation?

Wilbert

Dear Wilbert,

You are an empath, especially in the area of reproduction. There are a few past life moments attached to this but it is mostly your unique ability to "feel" the energy of a soul moving in and out of physical form.

When you are not physical you assist in the transitions to the mother's body. The nauseous feelings are the result of the energy vibration's intensity in that moment.

You have always participated in these vibrational moments, in and out of the physical.

-VERONICA

90

Dear VERONICA,

I got divorced about a year ago. I have been married 3 times. My question to you is I have heard it said that there is more than 1 soulmate for us - what do you believe about the idea of a soulmate(s)?

I am not sure I believe in marriage or soulmate(s) at this point in my life. Do you think these ideas are just accepted beliefs that have been past down from generation to generation?

Cheryl

Dear Cheryl,

From our perspective a soulmate is a romantic illusion created in the linear... often misleading to those seeking connection and devastating to the heart when it does not go smoothly.

A more accurate definition is to view all physical manifestation as a product of soul energy. This energy vibrating at different frequencies attracts other like vibration. Lessons, choices, and ego play the most important part in whether a linear relationship remains stable.

There are many similar energy matches, thus the concept of one soulmate is inaccurate.

-VERONICA

91

Dear VERONICA,

I have some concerns about my six year old son. I think he has been seeing spirits his whole life so far. He is fearful of his ability and his intuition. Is there anything I should know about him and how can I help him? Are we supposed to be teaching each other something?

Thank you, Emily

Dear Emily,

Engage him in conversation about what he feels and sees. Help to have a sense of normalcy about what is occurring.

He is an extremely sensitive energy that will likely retain his abilities into adulthood. He is opening up new avenues of perspective for you. And you are a great support system for him.

-VERONICA

92

Dear Veronica:

In great reluctance, I had to put my beloved dog Buddy to sleep today.

Unfortunately due to my financial situation I had to go to the humane society where they would not let me go back with him.

I am devastated because I know he was scared and so used to being abandoned.

I adopted him three years ago from a shelter. He was an older dog with a lot of issues but I gave him the best home I could for that time.

I would like to know if he is okay with the way I had to leave him.

I'm heartbroken and would like a little assurance that he understood. Also, was he met by my other dog Tugger?

Thank you for whatever assistance you can give my heart.

Sincerely,

Terri

Dear Terri,

Buddy was grateful for the stability you brought to his life. He was not afraid but energetically evolved by your energy.

He was aware of his biological issues and found comfort in his soul's release.

Yes. He was met by many energies... Tugger among them. Buddy was a highly evolved soul and loved you enormously.

-VERONICA

93

Dear Veronica,

After we die physically how long (in earth time?) do we wait before we incarnate again?

I heard that we often incarnate with the same family but that doesn't make a whole lot of sense to me.

For example, my sister Cathy died a few years ago. At the time of her death she was being greeted by our long time deceased grandmother.

I had a dream before my sister died and in that dream my grandmother told me not to worry about Cathy because she would take care of her.

Does this mean that my grandmother was waiting all this time for her? Or, in any other case could it be that we just keep moving along into one body right after another?

One last question: Is my sister Cathy still on the other side or has she incarnated again by now? Thank you!

Barbara

Dear Barbara,

Reincarnation is not a linear process. Most on the earth plane perceive it from that point of view, however. In the larger picture there is a multi-dimension aspect that is not being considered.

For example, one may incarnate in the American Revolution then move forward so to speak into the Middle Ages.... a difficult concept to comprehend while in the time-line.

No, your sister Cathy is still in contemplation with her guides. For her the measurement of time is now irrelevant while to you it's the basis of your current existence.

-VERONICA

94

Dear *VERONICA,*

After this present "linear" existence has changed into non physical, how do our opposing earthbound religious and political differences and indifference's meet up?

Is there common ground? Or do we find ourselves continuing with the particular present religious or political systems we may have embraced?

Douglas

Dear Douglas,

The linear choices of belief systems are attached to the linear life in hopes that by choosing them one will embark upon evolution.

However, it usually results in the belief systems interfering with the evolution of the soul.

Since there are multiple linear lives, the belief systems are ever evolving. The older the soul in experience the less influence the linear belief system has upon the life.

Ultimately the soul will become more involved in the process causing physical cognitive moments to be more discerning when choosing a belief system to become involved with.

-VERONICA

95

Dear VERONICA,

I would like to know if entities choose to reincarnate once they have reached the point of enlightenment?

Or, do those entities most always remain on the "other side"?

I would also like to know if all entities continue to reincarnate until they reach the point of enlightenment or are there other ways of reaching enlightenment without reincarnating and coming into the physical realm?

Thank you very much,

Valorie

Dear Valorie,

Energies who wish to can reincarnate, however, it is an individualistic moment, not to be judged by linear perspective.

Enlightenment is available from infinite sources.

Choosing the linear experience offers a condensed environment for lesser evolved souls and often more advanced ones.

It depends upon the free will of the energy involved.

-VERONICA

96

Dear VERONICA,

I have been in and out of relationships for many years and am still waiting for my soul mate to come in. The last couple years I have consulted a "seer" who described him in detail on several occasions. I am more than ready and wonder if I am doing something or not doing something to keep him from coming in. I've never felt like I was meant to be alone in this life.

I am ready---Cara

Dear Cara,

We suggest "seeing" him for yourself. To see him through another is not as powerful creatively as it should be.

Remember your thoughts create your reality. You are correct, your energy is ready. Open your eyes and "see".

-VERONICA

97

Dear VERONICA,

I believe souls choose what family they come into for growth opportunities and challenges. Does this also apply to children who are adopted? Did they intend to come into the family knowing they will eventually end up with another family? I have three adopted children after miscarriages failed my own pregnancies. Hugs, Judith

Dear Judith,

Children will find the appropriate energies to experience growth. Connection is spiritual and energetic, the physical body merely a vehicle to align correctly.

Your three children came in fully intending to be with you...the physical mother an instrument of love to get to the intended destination, most of which was pre-planned.

    -VERONICA

98

Editor's note: Because of the manner in which the following letter was written, VERONICA chose to reply to each question within the body of the letter rather than write a letter at the end as usual.

Dear VERONICA,

Thank You for Your Teachings.

I look forward to each one.

I have believed for a long time that we,our souls, have many "lives" but have always pondered the following questions. Would you please clarify?

1) Do we come back to live each life on this Earth or do we live in different "places"?

VERONICA: There are experiences available not only in a linear way but multi-dimensionally as well.

2) In different eras, like could I come back in say the Roman era after living in this era?

VERONICA: Yes reincarnation is not time-line dictated in order.

3) Do we connect with the same people/souls in each life, e.g. my daughter could be my father in another life? People we are very connected to in this life, do we connect again in each life?

VERONICA: There are overlaps of energies in each linear. In some cases the same groupings reincarnate "time after time" or perhaps skip a few for contemplation.

4) If one decides to end this life before the soul is finished experiencing everything it wants/needs to, will one relive the same life over?

VERONICA: You will always return to finish the lesson. Early endings (suicide) are not a free pass out of the current lesson. The soul will return to define the life.

Thank You for taking the time to consider my questions and thank you so very very much again for coming through to us and helping us understand who we really are.

Yours Sincerely,

Cynthea

VERONICA: You are quite welcome.

-VERONICA

99

Dear VERONICA,

I have a question I hope you can answer for me. It is the subject of "Re-Incarnation".

I have heard and read many pro's and con's on the subject, but none have given me a true, solid answer. I would appreciate it immensely if you could do that for me.

I always enjoy your answers to questions.

Regards,

- Marilyn

Dear Marilyn,

The idea of life from a complete linear perspective would be that it has a beginning and an end. That is true and solid from a purely documented experienced moment by many.

We offer for thought the multidimensional feelings by many, of the eternal base of the soul. If one lets their linear consciousness wander the experiences of other lifetimes do come forward. They can be dismissed of course but they do come forward.

Lifetimes vary in their lesson completeness, which is a true and solid statement. How unfortunate not to have another opportunity to participate.

We seek not to prove anything. It is only through evolvement that you will truly get your answer.

It is true that you are eternal.

It is true that your have multiple layers of experience.

It is true when you <u>decide</u> reincarnation is true.

-VERONICA

100

Dear Veronica,

How do you explain adoption? My girls were adopted from China and I always wonder how they were chosen for me...how did their souls find me?

Thank you, Patty from Connecticut

Dear Patty,

Adoption is a process where souls find the opportunity to connect in the physical with other souls. In most cases the biological system does not work out so the energy creates the path.

When a soul incarnates it is more complex than just a genetic experience. It is a multi-dimensional expression that can and will transcend all physical boundaries to be with the parent of choice.

-VERONICA

101

Dear VERONICA,

Can you describe your current surroundings in a way that I may comprehend, or better yet, remember?

Thanks, Deb

Dear Deb,

Our reality is a fluid environment that is created by thought construction. There are no linear laws that define it nor are they relevant.

There is a conscious vibration that resonates throughout our being and all that surrounds us. We are experiencing a true moment of "thought creates reality without the linear rules", in other words.

This is the most simplistic definition.

-VERONICA

102

Dear Veronica,

Is there suffering during the transition between lives for a person who is in severe physical distress such as Joan of Arc?   Thanks. Jean

Dear Jean,

Upon leaving the physical body form all distress is removed. The memory establishes itself in the form, however, suffering in that way is no longer relevant.

Whatever lessons or issues remain often are accompanied by guides who attempt to soothe the soul. There are many memories within the soul as it moves from experience to experience. It should be known that balance is applied so that the soul may glean the lesson involved.

-VERONICA

103

Dear VERONICA,

Do you find as much, or more, fulfillment, as an entity, in the form you are than when you were in the linear?

Thank you.

Patricia

Dear Patricia,

Yes, however, we find both to be of value. The complex energy we now participate in allows us the full viewpoint of all experience.

In the linear there were highly condensed experiences that involved our energy profoundly.

-VERONICA

104

Dear Veronica,

Hello, I was wondering when April goes into a trance, where does she go? Is she studying on some other plane herself, or does she just sit and be quiet while it's all happening?

Can she remember all that is said? I was just wondering what April gets out of all of this? Can she stop doing this if she chooses? With Love, Pamela

Editor's note: Since this question is about April, April decided to respond to it herself.

Dear Pamela,

I could stop doing this anytime I choose. Instead, being adventurous I choose not to. The opportunity presented itself when I was not quite prepared but over the years the energy connection is so unique and beautiful, that it's quite beyond anything I ever could have imagined.

While in trance it feels rather like a daydream. There are a variety of things that occur. If I am physically unwell there is a balancing of energy that realigns my health.

Sometimes I converse with interesting energies who have insights of interest. There are moments when I have a vague memory of what is being discussed during a session. Afterwards I may remember bits and pieces but they usually fade by the day's end.

I feel fortunate to be involved in such a process. There has never been a moment of fear, for the energies who speak through me are of sound countenance. They are friends of whom I am honored to know.

What do I get? A non-linear existence and perspective while still focused in the linear. More than I could have ever thought to wish for.

--April

105

Dear VERONICA,

What are your thoughts and suggestions on 2012?

One hears so much about it now, but really no one has suggestions how one can prepare or even if there is a preparation.

Thank you very much,

Vera

Dear Vera,

Linear measurement exists only in the linear. While there are indeed shifts of energy occurring in your perceptions, to assign a date is somewhat inaccurate.

We say that consciousness and the way it participates in its reality evolves, however, that does not mean that it ends.

Proclamations of doom are perhaps a bit exaggerated. It would be more relevant to become engaged in the shifts so that the transition is of a smoother nature.

Evolvement consists of shedding old ways and energies. This may appear extremely negative from the linear eye in the moment, however, once the energy settles the results will be better than expected.

Perhaps by allowing the negative to disassemble itself while creating in your thoughts moments of connection and prosperity, these allowing's will translate to the earth plane of which you inhabit.

Perhaps it is not the end but the beginning of a good moment.

-VERONICA

Dear Veronica,

Why did we, who are energies that could exist eternally in spiritual dimensions, choose in the first place, to incarnate on Earth?

W.M.

Dear W.M.,

The Earth plane as you know it is an opportunity for your energy to experience whatever it is most curious about. The dense reality offers a perception not available within spiritual dimensions.

There are those who participate who may have another more negative opinion about the physical plane but it should be considered that to really "know" something, one should experience both the positive and negative. This offers complete understanding.

If one remembers to look at physical from a multi-life perspective, on can see the full rounded approach. However, most view life from a single perspective and may become depressed or angry if the current experience is more negative in nature.

--VERONICA

106

Dear VERONICA,

After viewing your latest video on YouTube, I got the message: We are essentially full divinity dressed up in flesh bodies, but we are deceived by our ego into thinking that we are only the body.

Can we manifest our true nature, our divinity, while we are encased in our mantle of flesh? If we can, what must we do to make this possible. W.M.

Dear W.M.,

As stated in the previous answer, we repeat that it is necessary to view existence from a multi-life perspective.

Your evolution is a grand novel of expression. To read only one chapter is an inaccurate assessment of the full story.

-VERONICA

107

Dear Veronica,

I have read all the Edgar Casey books and I have always had a question about reincarnation. When someone dies and his spirit is ready to reincarnate, can he or would he reincarnate as someone in another world or dimension?

We are always concerned with his coming back in this world as a human, but really, if he chooses to, he can decide a totally alien form. Is that true?

Thanks, John, NY City

Dear John,

The option is surely available but not always a common choice.

-VERONICA

108

Dear Veronica,

My husband passed away November 11, 2006.

We were married 35 years and I think of him every day. I have on walking my dog, started talking to another widow, and somehow I think we like one another.

I meet him once a week on my walks, and I think, I am only 58, and what would my husband on the other side think?

I know its up to me, but could you tell me in this situation what once happily married spouses on the other side think?

Do they know?

Please tell me.

--Maureen

Dear Maureen,

Partners who move to spirit often send other appropriate souls to keep their love ones comforted in the physical.

Your husband wishes your remaining years to be full. He knows well this arrangement and is happy for your increased energy and contentment.

-VERONICA

109

Dear VERONICA,

Can you clarify for me as I am confused as to is it predetermined when we are to leave the earth? Or do we have a say depending on how we treat our chosen body? Can we lengthen the time we spend here? And are our lifestyle choices a deciding factor?

For I have been of the feeling that I will die at a certain age of 63. Is this just my thought's creation? Am I copping out? Thank you. Signed Pat

Dear Pat,

There is a plan in place implemented by yourself. It can be altered by your choices as you make your way through the linear experience. We say that 63 was an optional exit, however, whatever you choose moving forward will determine the accuracy.

-VERONICA

110

Dear Veronica:

Do you feel that individuals are born homosexual and that they don't have a choice about it?

My son is struggling with this. He is fearful that he might be gay and although he does not want to be, he feels that he doesn't have a choice.

I feel that he does have a choice and is just confused, and that his fearful thoughts could create this reality. What do you think?

Julie

Dear Julie,

All energies are both male/female in spirit with one or the other being more predominant.

It is the intention of the soul to manifest both genders in the physical during the reincarnational cycle. Often there are those who being, for example, very male, find themselves manifested in a female body... and the opposite.

Your son is a warrior energy that is more female than male in focus. The intention was to participate in a male life; however, the energy is finding it difficult.

It is not a simple dilemma for him. His warrior energy feels like the male experience is important but the dominant female part of him questions that.

Love your son regardless of the final decision and allow his soul to make the choice. He will find the correct path. He is not fearful of his soul. Advise him to follow his soulful energy... and remain neutral.

This is his process and he will determine his path. His greatest fear is your opinion of him.

-VERONICA

111

Dear Veronica,

Will we all have the opportunity to one day do what you do and help people on earth?

Thanks for your consideration and please forgive the humanness of my inquiry! Many thanks,

Loving Hopeful, from Orange

Dear Orange,

All souls when leaving the physical plane move through an assessment of their previous life.

If at that moment they feel there will be more advancement for others and themselves, they will leave the reincarnational cycle to assist others as we do. It is a conscious choice.

-VERONICA

112

Hi Veronica,

I enjoy your newsletter and I was also thrilled with a reading that your did for me recently.

Could you please explain what linear time, thought, logic....means?

I gather it is not seeing the big picture, but we do work with past, present and future concepts.

What is the purpose of all living things existing in linear time?

It seems that all of our problems stem from being linear.

Thank you,

J.B.

Dear J.B.,

Linear time is a measurement of existence while in the condensed physical reality.

Perception of that participation is based in thought.

Logic is the mind's way of defining thought.

Linear time is an opportunity to have an intense energetic experience and is considered a gift by those who are in Spirit.

Problems in the linear are created to be overcome while attempting to have a better understanding of the soul.

--VERONICA

113

Dear VERONICA,

What are we when we die?

I believe the personality we have on the Earth Plane is just for that lifetime.

So when I Mary-Kathryn die so does my body and my personality.

So what am I, when I die?

I can't be Mary Kathryn.

Dear Mary Kathryn,

   The multiplicity of all the experiences of your soul remain with you.

Outside of the physical timeline this is an easier concept to understand. You have been a Paul, Ryma, Little Bear, Patricia and Alyahah to name a few.

All of those experiences remain vivid in the thoughts of your soul eternally.

When you leave the earth plane all of your personalities merge but do not diminish.

You are your soul, which never dies.

Mary-Kathryn is but a singular journey in the expansiveness of your soul.

-VERONICA

114

Dear VERONICA,

I am curious of your feelings towards animals and their intelligence. In your senses, do you feel they are capable of creating art ?

Art is an expression of intelligence. Horses are highly intelligent. I am certain my horse is intentionally creating art. Renee

Dear Renee,

We know the existence of artful talent in what you perceive as the animal kingdom. Like humans, different animal incarnations have artistic talents while others excel in other arenas.

The expression is not limited to horses, however, we do agree yours has a gift.

-VERONICA

115

Dear VERONICA,

I tried to save a badly crippled kitten.

She tried so hard to survive that I did not have the heart to terminate her. Her brain had been affected by her mother's illness and she had no co-ordination.

Eventually she could not displace herself at all. I think I'm responsible for forcing her to take a cat's fortifier that gave bad diarrhea. That's when she lost whatever balance she had.

I had to have her put down.

Does she know how much I love and miss her, and does she forgive me my stupidity? Thank you.

Tery

Dear Tery,

Animals are highly evolved energies participating in a linear life just as you are. The inability for a kitten to express itself in human language does not diminish its ability to comprehend.

This was all about participating in the giving of yourself unconditionally in response to the desire of your soul to evolve.

The kitten energy thrives, delighted to be a part of your journey. You will see her again, perhaps under more prolonged linear circumstances.

Your perceived self stupidity only enhanced the relationship. This is a long term relationship spanning many lives.

Look for her for she will be seeking your energy again soon.

-VERONICA

116

Dear Veronica:

I am very upset right now as I watch over my aged mother. She is very independent and wants to live her own life, but I am seeing lots of examples of her encroaching dementia, and an inability to make good, sound decisions.

The situation has become more complicated by a man who is insinuating himself into her life. I am very ill at ease with the situation.

How can I support my mother, and at the same time keep her safe?

I know there is a lesson here, but I am having a hard time finding the positive. My mind is totally consumed with all the negative possibilities.... Please help me.

Susan

Dear Susan,

Perhaps the consuming negativity in the thoughts of your mind are the ultimate culprit. Decide to take all the drama out of the situation for a moment.

The examples are but a result of your own fears concerning your mother. Realize, while deteriorating physically, her soul is acting in her favor. The fellow in question has the probability of becoming a so called victim of her encroaching dementia.

The lesson is that your mother will resolve the issue with her own soulful power. Be there, as her daughter, support her without fear. Understand that not all negativity may gain a foothold in a life. By being fearful you are supporting the gentleman in question.

Decide to be positive spiritually. By that participation your mother will have better opportunity to be successful.

-VERONICA

117

Dear VERONICA,

I have a question. In the newest "Inner Whispers" that I received today, you said that at the time of assessment of its life the soul can opt out of the reincarnational cycle.

Does that mean you would never have the chance to reincarnate again? Thanks. Sue

Dear Sue,

The reincarnational process is available at all times to the soul. In choosing to opt out of the cycle, it does not mean the choice is no longer within reach.

Often a soul chooses to do other things for a while in an effort to evolve. There is no such moment as never in the eternal... So the choice will remain available if the soul chooses.

-VERONICA

118

Dear VERONICA,

Hello, I have a couple of questions on 'time'. Hopefully you can give me some guidance on the subject to see if I am understanding it right.

In our lives we see time as running horizontally forward (if that makes sense). But really if there is no time, is this right?

Also - In my next life I choose, it can be set for any time period on earth. For example: If I think the 1400'S would be the best time period for my energy to learn something specific. I can choose it.

I don't have to come back in the future. I don't have to follow the timeline because there really isn't one.

Am I understanding it properly? THANK YOU VERY MUCH FOR YOUR "TIME". Patty

Dear Patty,

Yes my dear you are.

Linear perception of linear is just that.... a perception.

One can choose to move to any time period they choose.

It is not a process dictated by a timeline.

From this life in the early 2000's one might decide to incarnate in 1200 AD. Or, even 1200 BC.

The opportunity for growth determines the stage where one will choose to "live" to evolve.

-VERONICA

119

Dear Veronica,

I get the message that love is important; but what exactly is the meaning of this love?

It has different meanings to us here, I assume it means different things to you there. On the other side, there isn't all the daily maintenance that there is here, or is there?

To me, love means I take care of someone; maintenance is the name of the game in this life. To me, love means I surround someone with my thoughts of protection.

To me, love means enjoying someone's company.

To me, love is a connection that actively feels good.

What does love mean to you?

Your Friend, Chloe

Dear Chloe,

Love is an expression of connection without any conditions.

Outside of the linear love expands to what you would term as infinity.

There is a beginning, however, there is no end once it is discovered.

The discovery of love is the key to many things.

-VERONICA

120

Dear VERONICA,

You say there is no linear, no time in your place, yet you talk about older or younger souls. How do souls come to be, are they born, or created?

Then again if there is no linear time in your place, how can anything be younger or older? --- Anonymous

Dear Anonymous,

Souls are cast from source entities or their aspects, thus definition of being born is a bit out of line with the eternal moment.

Being born is usually a physical definition of creation.

Time exists only in the physical realm. Outside of physical the idea of time is not necessary since all participation can be very multiplistic.

We refer to younger and older souls merely as a reference to those of you listening in the linear. Existence is multi-dimensional and expansive.

There are experiences that happen simultaneously that allow for some souls to have greater evolution. Thus the term older soul applies. A younger soul is one who is cast but has a different experience level than an older soul... perhaps with a more singular experience than one who has multi-dimensional experiences.

It is indeed difficult to understand the eternal through lines and language. Everything in the eternal is vibratory.

Love is an expression of connection without any conditions.

-VERONICA

Editor's note: The use of the word "multiplistic" is intentional with that spelling.

121

Dear Veronica,

I am curious why we haven't gotten to know about April.

I am in awe of her ability to shift aside and allow you to come into her being in every way.

Is she shy, extremely private about her life, or doesn't see that it's about her at all?

Is April sometimes amazed at the things Veronica says because she is not aware of what's coming out of her mouth when she's channeling?

Thank you!

Betsy

Dear Betsy,

We began our relationship with the April Crawford many years ago by your standards.

She does not participate in the process other than to lend her physical for our expression. Indeed she is aware it is not about her.

The process brings awareness on many different levels for many people incarnate. To keep the integrity of the work pure she does not listen to most of the sessions. She feels that the separation is necessary to the work.

We are in agreement.

-VERONICA

***

About the Author

April Crawford is an AMAZON Top 50 Best Selling Author, but April is also one of the world's most naturally talented and adept Open Deep Trance Channels and Spiritual Mediums.

April Crawford is Internationally known as both an author and as an Open Deep Trance Channel and Spiritual Medium, with clients in most countries of the world.

April's spiritual newsletter, *"Inner Whispers"*, is written by highly evolved nonphysical entities and guides and is read by tens of thousands of readers each week. It is available (free) at www.InnerWhispers.net

~ About the Author ~

April currently lives in Los Angeles, California with her husband, Allen, and her many pets

***

OTHER BOOKS
BY
APRIL CRAWFORD

"Inner Whispers":

Messages From A Spirit Guide (Volume I)

Available also as Kindle Book

www.InnerWhispersTheBook.com

"Inner Whispers":

Messages From A Spirit Guide (Volume II)

Available also as Kindle Book

www.InnerWhispersTheBook.com

"Parting Notes": A Connection With The Afterlife

Also available as a Kindle Book

www.PartingNotes.com

Other Books by April Crawford

Ashram Tang... a Story... and a Discovery

Available also as a Kindle Book.

www.AshramTang.com

Reflections of a Spiritual Astronaut: Book I

Available as a Kindle Book.

Reflections of a Spiritual Astronaut: Book II

Available as a Kindle Book.

your life and its choices: THE RECIPE FOR ASCENTION TO ANOTHER PLANE "A" TO "Z"

By Ish and Osco (Spirit Guides) via April Crawford

Available as a Kindle Book.

Deep Trance Channeling Sessions:
Special Edition No.1

Available as a Kindle Book

For more information about the Author or about True Open Deep Trance Channeling:

www.AprilCrawford.com

Other Books by April Crawford

For the free spiritual newsletter *"Inner Whispers"*
www.InnerWhispers.net

For personal telephone or in-person consultations
via April Crawford, Personal Appearances, or
Media Interviews contact Allen at
AprilReadings@aol.com

***

www.ingramcontent.com/pod-product-compliance
Lightning Source LLC
LaVergne TN
LVHW051503080426
835509LV00017B/1892